CLOAK OF SECRECY

CLOAK OF SECRECY

◆

The Special Cults of the Ontario Government

"Our experiences as a small landlord and how we learned that there is no accountability by the government or its low-income clients."

Charles Arthur, Ph.D.
Eileen Gwyneth Roy

iUniverse, Inc.
New York Lincoln Shanghai

CLOAK OF SECRECY
The Special Cults of the Ontario Government

iUniverse books may be ordered through booksellers or by contacting:

iUniverse
2021 Pine Lake Road, Suite 100
Lincoln, NE 68512
www.iuniverse.com
1-800-Authors (1-800-288-4677)

Because of the dynamic nature of the Internet, any Web addresses or links contained in this book may have changed since publication and may no longer be valid.

The views expressed in this work are solely those of the author and do not necessarily reflect the views of the publisher, and the publisher hereby disclaims any responsibility for them.

ISBN: 978-0-595-45103-6 (pbk)
ISBN: 978-0-595-89415-4 (ebk)

Printed in the United States of America

This book is dedicated to "Jessica"

We saw you, standing there
Shy and delicate
Big brown eyes, long brown hair
Looking mysteriously out of place ...
Too much hustle and bustle for you, for us
Too many people coming and going, always busy
Not noticing you, only us, we watched you ...
Where's your mommy? Where's your daddy?
Too high ... too high ... only themselves they care ...
Time goes by ... we see you asking sweetly
"Can I help you?" We smile ... yes
You helped us while others had their parties
Curious, we remember
Big brown eyes, long brown hair
Looking mysteriously out of place
We worry how you are ... are you safe?
Too sweet to have fallen
Like those who surround you
We watched, we wondered, we cared
Eight years old. Do others care?

Eileen Gwyneth Roy

Contents

Foreword

In this book we draw on our experience providing rental housing for low-income tenants, to expose deep-seated flaws in Ontario's social welfare and landlord-tenant systems that pose a real threat to the social, economic and political stability of the province. For example, among the experiences we relate is a clear failure by the Windsor children's aid society (CAS) described in Chapter 6.

We have owned rental properties in Windsor, Ontario for over ten years. We are ordinary, middle-aged, middle-class working people. Initially we were very excited about the prospect of buying small rental properties, fixing them up, and renting them out. It was a chance to improve the properties and provide a valuable service for people, while building a successful business. With retirement from our regular jobs looming within ten years, we saw it as an opportunity to keep active and generate some extra income well into retirement.

We had heard horror stories, some first hand, others from newspapers or magazines, about small landlords victimized by "professional tenants" who were able to live rent-free for months. We were sure that these problems must be the result of major mistakes made by these landlords, not a failing of the landlord-tenant system. In some of the cases, acquaintances had rented out their house when they had been transferred to another city. When a tenant stopped paying rent, these landlords failed to take quick action to evict the freeloaders, and suffered the consequences. It seemed clear to us that the losses suffered by these landlords were their own fault, not a systemic problem. No system is foolproof, but only a small number of tenants would possess the level of expertise needed to perpetrate a major scam, we reasoned. We were anxious to tackle the challenge of owning a rental property and prove that we could outsmart anyone who might try to take advantage of us.

In business, it is important to be able to measure the consequences of every activity. Financial performance is an important yardstick. There are other, more subjective measures, such as the satisfaction of providing an essential service to customers. By any measure, our rental operation has been an abject failure. Looking back, we should not be surprised that this promising enterprise did not turn out as we envisaged it. The deck was stacked against us from the beginning.

In this book, we analyze the root causes of the difficulties our rental operation has faced. We show that much of the responsibility for these problems lies with the Ontario landlord-tenant and welfare systems. We describe actual events and experiences that have occurred over the years to illustrate how far the government has tilted the playing field in favour of tenants, particularly low-income tenants, and especially those who receive social assistance. Names have been changed in the interest of privacy. Some of these anecdotes are funny, some are pathetic, and some are funny *and* pathetic. Social activists or others with an axe to grind may dismiss them as the usual tenant horror stories that everyone has heard before. However, we believe that they are symptomatic of serious social, political and economic problems, which are dragging down cities across Ontario and, ultimately, threaten the comfortable middle class existence enjoyed by the majority of Ontarians.

The real life stories naturally lead to discussions of the systematic and systemic problems engendered by the province's landlord-tenant and social welfare systems, which plague the rental housing sector. We shed some light on the workings of the Ontario welfare system, a system that is a complete mystery to the majority of Ontarians. We also examine the causes of Windsor's decline, and show how geopolitical developments and Canada-US relations have had a profound impact on the city.

We probe the myths and realities that shape the underpinnings of the system. We show that those who promote the myths that help to perpetuate the current dysfunctional system are benefiting from it, and stand to prosper even more as a misinformed public ignores ongoing harmful changes.

We are not so naive as to think that publishing this book can lead to changes in the social welfare system. However, we hope it will help to increase public awareness. At least, it should be of interest to those who are curious about this little-understood aspect of life in Ontario. Perhaps it may stimulate investigations of the welfare system by others who have the resources and the expertise to drive change. Most importantly, it provides invaluable information, and a clear warning, for anyone who is contemplating becoming a small landlord in Ontario in general, and in Windsor in particular.

1

The Welfare Trap: Government Cost Cutting at the Landlords' Expense

Any owner of affordable rental housing in Windsor has had tenants who are receiving social assistance. There are about 10,000 families in Windsor receiving social assistance[1], in a city with a total population of just over 200,000. The concentration of people receiving social assistance in the downtown area of Windsor is much higher since these people tend to gravitate to this area. Low mortgage rates have enticed lower middle class families and even the working poor to purchase homes, leaving the clients of the welfare system to make up the bulk of the tenant population.

The average middle-class Ontarian is probably vaguely aware of some facts about the welfare system. For example, it's generally well known that there are a number of different kinds of social assistance depending on the status of the recipient. Many people know that mother's allowance payments were cut 22 percent by the Mike Harris government in the 1990s and were subsequently frozen for nine years. They may also realize that welfare was downloaded from the provincial government to local governments by the Harris government. Beyond these political and policy-level issues, which crop up in the newspapers periodically, the workings of the welfare system remain a mystery to

---

1. Based on the 2005 City of Windsor social services operating expenditure of $206 million, assuming an average expenditure of $20,000 per family per year.

the general public. They remain largely a mystery to us, even though as landlords we have been dealing with Windsor social services and its clients on a continuous basis for the past ten years.

Whether this admitted ignorance on our part could be rectified by more research is an open question, but it is undeniably true that the welfare system is cloaked in secrecy and gives every appearance of being, to paraphrase former Ontario Power Generation chairman Bill Farlinger, "some sort of special welfare cult." Like the Branch Davidians, or any of the other well-known religious cults, the welfare system, including the social services apparatus and their "clients" represents a way of life unfamiliar to the majority of people, and to be avoided like the plague. The practitioners follow a system of rules mostly known only to them, and contact with outsiders is avoided as much as possible. High walls protect the "compound," lest the wrong people gain access. In spite of our imperfect understanding of the system, we will at least shine some light through whatever cracks are in the walls.

The purpose of social assistance is theoretically to provide temporary help to those who are capable of working but have fallen on hard times through no fault of their own, and to assist those who are not capable of working. The principle is that the general working population funds this assistance through taxes. This seems reasonable; an alternative would be for those who need help to rely on charity as was done in the past, but most Ontarians prefer that the needy should be entitled to assistance rather than having to depend on charity.

While the principle is sound, its practical implementation is problematic. Most people would rather not have to work forty hours a week if it was not required to maintain a reasonable lifestyle. We're not talking about the kind of lifestyle that follows winning the lottery—many people would accept a very modest lifestyle in return for not having to work. If one's earning potential in the marketplace is limited to the minimum wage, it's tempting to forego an occasional extra visit to Tim Horton's in exchange for the luxury of being able to shop during weekdays when there are no crowds in the stores. So as a practical matter, the welfare system should be able to differentiate between those who really cannot work or find a job, and those who are tempted to obtain welfare just to avoid working.

The system attempts to address this problem by setting eligibility rules, and by keeping welfare payments low. If someone meets the eligibility rules, he or she is entitled to welfare payments. The low payments are ostensibly intended to discourage able-bodied individuals from applying for welfare, but they also serve a more important political purpose of minimizing complaints from the taxpayers who are footing the bill to support welfare recipients. They also allow the government to keep the minimum wage low, thereby placating business interests.

If welfare payments are to be kept low, how are welfare recipients to be housed? In the recent past, government policy was to provide public housing for these people. Large housing projects were funded and constructed by the government. Construction costs were minimized by economies of scale and by avoiding frills. Operating costs were minimized, since the owner (the government) made no profit. Costs were also kept down by under-maintaining the properties. Low-income tenants can be hard on a property, and by not carrying out proper maintenance governments are now saddled with huge bills to repair or rebuild public housing.

A November 25, 2005 article in the *Toronto Star* titled "Tenants to Pick Lord of Slums," describes a campaign by the Parkdale Tenant's Association of Toronto to draw attention to bad rental conditions. An official of the Toronto Community Housing Corporation is quoted as saying the tenant's association is guilty of giving an "extremely inaccurate portrayal" of public housing conditions in Parkdale. "It doesn't recognize any of the investments we've made despite being cash-strapped" he said, adding $600,000 has been spent over the last two years on a cluster of buildings in Parkdale.

Unfortunately, $600,000 over two years is peanuts for a landlord that is operating 58,000 units. It amounts to about $5.00 per unit, per year. Perhaps the Toronto Community Housing Corporation benefits from economies of scale, but it's still hard to believe that anything meaningful can be done at that level of spending, or that compliance with building, fire, electrical, and health codes can be maintained. Our experience has been that of the order of at least $1,000 per unit, per year is required in repairs and maintenance just to maintain the condition of a property.

About ten years ago, governments stopped building social housing. Privately owned housing has been relied upon to take up the slack. But how can housing provided by the open market be guaranteed to be affordable? Landlords have costs such as utilities, taxes, insurance, building materials, and labour, which have to be covered by rents in order to stay in business. We all know how unstable these costs are. As landlords have tried to recoup their costs through higher rents, tenant groups have been formed to lobby governments for rent controls and other restrictions on rental operations. Although rents have fallen over the last couple of years in most Ontario cities, tenant groups continue to complain that landlords should be forced to provide more affordable housing.

It's worth noting that social housing agencies won't rent to someone who has previously stiffed public housing. For example, Windsor Housing bars a household if anyone in the household owes rent arrears to any Federally, Provincially, or Municipally funded housing group in Ontario (unless they are following an approved repayment schedule). These less-than-ideal renters are cut loose from the public housing sector to swell the ranks of the tenant pool available to private landlords.

In a world where housing costs are rapidly rising but welfare payments are tightly controlled, how can these two opposing trends be reconciled? How can rental accommodation be made affordable for low-income tenants in an environment of ever-rising costs? Based on our experience as owners of rental properties in Windsor, it is clear to us that the government's answer has been to operate the welfare system, the landlord-tenant system, and city inspections so as to transfer money from landlords to tenants. In effect, the market rents charged by landlords are partially clawed back to the tenants by the system. The provincial and local governments work in unison to achieve this result.

The most important vehicle for transferring money from landlords to social assistance recipients is the eviction process. There is a lot of sympathy among the general public for welfare families that get evicted from their homes because they are unable to pay their rent. The evil landlord has long been an accepted image in books, movies and the news media. However, this image and the corresponding unwavering sympathy for tenants are badly misplaced in this day and age. The fact is that nowadays most clients of social services benefit financially from being evicted, at the expense of their landlord. These tenants have a strong incentive to get themselves evicted, and many of them act accordingly.

The first way that a tenant benefits financially from being evicted is the prolonged and expensive eviction process mandated by the Residential Tenancies Act (formerly the Tenant Protection Act) and enforced by the Landlord and Tenant Board (formerly known as the Ontario Rental Housing Tribunal). If a tenant fails to pay her rent on the first of the month, she can legally remain in the rental unit for at least seven weeks even if she pays no rent and doesn't have a leg to stand on. If she hasn't paid last month's rent she can easily pocket almost two month's rent.

How is this possible? Well, if a tenant doesn't pay her rent on the first of the month, the landlord is entitled to serve an N4 "Notice to Terminate Early for Nonpayment of Rent." The N4 gives the tenant fourteen days to pay the rent, or she must move out. Does this mean she has to move out by the sixteenth of the month? No, all the landlord can do if she doesn't move out is file an L1 "Application to Terminate a Tenancy for Nonpayment of Rent and for Collection of Arrears of Rent" with the Landlord and Tenant Board (or "the Board," for short), which can be done on the seventeenth at the earliest. The landlord must pay the Board $150 to file the L1. If the seventeenth is a Saturday, the L1 must be filed on the following Monday, the nineteenth. If the nineteenth is a statutory holiday, it must be filed on the twentieth.

On the date that the L1 is filed by the landlord, the Board sets a hearing date which is normally three weeks or more after the date the L1 is filed, i.e. on or after the seventh of the following month. The Board issues a "Notice of Hearing" to the landlord. The landlord is then required to provide the tenant with a copy of the L1 and the Notice of Hearing. The landlord is also required to file a "Notice of Service" with the Board, indicating how and when the L1 and Notice of Hearing were provided to the Tenant.

Prior to implementation of the Residential Tenancies Act in February 2007, the tenant was given five calendar days to dispute the L1 to the Tribunal, in writing. Most tenants didn't bother to dispute the L1. After the five day dispute period expired the Tribunal would issue an Order to the tenant and the landlord (this would be on the twenty-sixth of the month in the best-case scenario) stating that the rent must be paid by a certain date (eleven calendar days from the date of the Order), or the landlord may apply to the sheriff on the following day to physically evict the tenant. Assuming the month has thirty days, the landlord would be able to apply to the sheriff on the eighth of the following month. The sheriff would schedule a visit to the property to evict the tenant a week or more later, i.e. on the fifteenth at the earliest. The sheriff's fee in Windsor is $325, and is not refundable if the tenant leaves before the sheriff arrives.

If the tenant were still in the unit on the eviction date, the sheriff would physically evict the tenant and post a notice on the door, giving the tenant 48 hours to remove her belongings.

One of the most important changes made in February 2007 is that the Board no longer has the option of issuing an Order without first holding a hearing. Under the Tribunal, if the tenant disputed the L1, a hearing would be held three weeks or more after the date the L1 is filed, i.e. on or after the seventh of the following month. Under the Board, there is no requirement for the tenant to dispute the L1, and a hearing *must* be held. Assuming that the landlord prevails at the hearing, the sheriff would evict the tenant on the fifteenth of the second month, or later. Realistically, it takes at least one week more than this timeline indicates, when holidays and other slippages in the process are accounted for. Therefore, it is realistic for the tenant to expect to stay until after the twentieth of the second month.

It's also worth noting that under the new rules, the tenant is entitled to raise maintenance issues at the eviction hearing. This gives a tenant the opportunity to argue that the landlord has not maintained her home properly, and that a rent abatement should be awarded to the tenant. If a rent abatement is awarded by the Board, and if it is sufficient to cover the unpaid rent, the tenant can stay. Furthermore, there is no guarantee that the tenant will pay her rent for the third month, and she may continue to argue that the repairs have not been made, further extending her rent-free stay.

Assuming that the unit is in good repair, at least the landlord has established an open and shut case, and can get a judgment against the tenant and recoup the unpaid rent plus court costs and sheriff's fees, right? Wrong! If the tenant is on social assistance, there is no way to get anything back. By law, social assistance payments cannot be garnisheed, and these tenants generally do not have a bank account. The money, which is rightfully owed to the landlord, is gone and is never coming back.

The second way in which a tenant who is a client of social services benefits from being evicted, at least in Windsor, is that social services generally pays her a "start-up fee" to get her going in a new place. If the tenant were to voluntarily move, with all rent owing to the previous landlord paid in full, she would not receive a start-up fee. Presumably she's not entitled to anything because it's her own decision to move. However, if the tenant is evicted for whatever reason, she is regarded as a victim by social services and is given a start-up fee. Therefore, social services provides tenants with an incentive to stop paying their rent and get themselves evicted. We consider this to be a direct attack by a government agency on one segment of society (landlords) on behalf of another (tenants). It is a shameful abuse of social service's responsibility.

The net result of all this is that many clients of social services tend to stay at one place for only a few months before they stop paying their rent and get themselves evicted. The financial loss to the landlord is far greater than the money gained by the tenant. In addition to losing the rent owed by the tenant, the landlord has to pay Board and sheriff's fees totaling $475. The landlord is unable to show the unit to prospective tenants until after the tenant is evicted and the unit can be cleaned and repaired, resulting in the loss of at least one more month's rent. To add insult to injury, tenants who move frequently generally own junky furniture, which they leave behind. It can cost several hundred dollars just to haul the junk to the City Dump.

We are reluctant to characterize tenants' behaviour as abusive, because they are basically handed the opportunity to live rent-free at their landlord's expense on a silver platter by the landlord-tenant and social welfare system. In a sense, who could blame them? Nevertheless, we don't want to leave the impression that all tenants behave this way. Some tenants actually pay their rent on time and give the required sixty days notice if they are planning to leave. Based on our experience, about half of low-income tenants are "good" and the rest are "bad." Sadly, the bad tenants (and, by extension, the government) are taking advantage of the good tenants as well as the landlords. Rents are higher than they need to be because of the bad tenants, and, because of the financial losses caused by bad tenants, landlords struggle to provide an adequate level of service to their good tenants.

Tenants automatically receive the benefits we've described above without doing anything or taking any action. All that's required of them is that they physically leave when the sheriff shows up at their door. However, woe is the landlord who slips up in any detail of the process. We recently observed a Tribunal hearing in which the landlord was seeking to evict a prostitute from a small building. The landlord had a letter from one of the other tenants stating that the prostitute's customers were disturbing the building at all hours of the night. The tenant had not arrived at the allotted time for the hearing so rather than make a judgment on the open and shut case, the Tribunal Adjudicator decided to wait and see if the tenant would show up. Half an hour later the prostitute showed up with a very large, intimidating man, and a legal aid lawyer in tow. On cross-examination of the landlord it turned out that she had taped the notice to the tenant on the tenant's door. That is not a prescribed method of notifying a tenant, and the case was thrown out. Most likely, the landlord and the "good" tenants have been sufficiently intimidated that the hooker can continue to conduct her business as she sees fit for a good long time.

We've made the case that the eviction process is slanted in favour of tenants. It's clear that one reason for this is an underlying assumption within governments and social services that landlords are absolutely responsible for their tenants. A seemingly minor feature of Tribunal/Board hearings illustrates this. We have observed several Tribunal hearings in which the tenant did not appear for the hearing and the landlord presented an open and shut case that the tenant had not paid her rent and should be evicted. After all of the evidence had been presented and the landlord had wrapped up her case, the Tribunal adjudicator asked the landlord if she knew of any reason why the tenant should not be evicted. In other words, if the tenant is vulnerable, the landlord is morally and legally bound to reveal that information. The adjudicator would then rule that the tenant could stay for an additional period of time, until she could get back on her feet. The landlord would be credited for the rent owed, but of course the collection of that rent is left up to the landlord and is unenforceable.

We're not well-versed in the reasons that require the landlord to volunteer the information that could lead to a ruling that a tenant cannot be evicted. However, it is clearly an extraordinary responsibility that is placed on the landlord, given the quasi-judicial setting of the Board. In any other court proceeding, each party would be expected and assumed to defend herself, and a party would not be asked or expected *by the judge* to volunteer information detrimental to the case. In a city where the vacancy rate has been over 10 percent for several years, how can a landlord be forced to keep a tenant rent-free?

We are not opposed to the principle that low income Ontarians are entitled to housing, but we do object to the current approach taken by government to achieve this objective. The issue is personal responsibility. On one hand, the government says that tenants have to take personal responsibility for making their rent payments and behaving as responsible citizens. Tenants are supposedly responsible for rectifying any shortfall in rent payments, and social services will not come to the rescue with a rent payment if there is a dispute with the landlord. On the other hand, clients of social services are handed all sorts of benefits on a platter. In addition to receiving the regular monthly payments to which they are entitled, they also receive a substantial start-up fee when they move to a new home, they are given free legal aid, and, most importantly, their social services payments cannot be garnisheed by the landlord. In reality, these tenants are not required to exercise any personal responsibility for their actions. Responsibility is loaded onto the backs of landlords, taxpayers, and the public at large.

While it is clear that the public has a responsibility to all of its citizens through government, we believe that this "culture of entitlement" is having serious consequences for all Ontarians, which go far beyond the obvious unfairness towards landlords.

An observation we have made which goes beyond the landlord-tenant relationship is that the system encourages young women receiving social assistance to continue having children on a regular basis. In a city like Windsor, young women in their mid to late teens, who may not have had an opportunity or inclination to acquire an adequate education or training, have two options: work in the sex industry, or go on welfare. Some do both. A young woman who rejects the sex industry has an immediate incentive to have a baby—her welfare payments will increase dramatically, both through the mother's allowance and the child tax credit. Equally important, from her perspective, is the fact that she will not be forced to go out to work for at least eighteen months. However, after eighteen months she will be asked to take job training or go out to work.

Fortunately there is a solution to that problem: have another baby. We have had several young tenants, and there are many more young women in Windsor, who have had three or four children by their mid-twenties in order to avoid working. There are plenty of young men who are willing to help these women conceive a child. Raising the child is another story. The vast majority of these young biological fathers soon disappears, or maintains a relationship with the young mother that is abusive, violent, and disruptive to the development of the child. As a result, in many low-income families each sibling has a different father.

In a country such as Canada, which has a very low birthrate—lower than what is required to just maintain the population—this incentive for the poorest and the least-educated to have children may be deliberate government policy. Clearly, governments would have to provide astronomical financial incentives to cause a meaningful increase in the birthrate among middle class women. However, there are obvious questions about how the children of the low-income "baby boom" are being raised and what the implications are for Ontario's future. It's clear that most children raised in poverty will never escape poverty, and will never contribute much to the mainstream economy. Why would governments encourage the creation and perpetuation of a significant segment of society that can only be a drain on the middle class? Perhaps governments regard low-income citizens as a kind of "spinning reserve;" a kind of insurance against labour shortages, or fodder for the military.

As we've said, the Ontario middle class are only vaguely aware of how the welfare system works, and probably don't want to know. The welfare bureaucracy takes advantage of this attitude and the ignorance that it engenders by maintaining a labyrinthine system designed to benefit the insiders.

Based on our experience, there are a few reforms to the welfare system, and to landlord-tenant law, which we feel should be implemented.

To address fairness towards landlords (and responsible tenants) in the face of widespread abuse by tenants, while maintaining fairness towards tenants and preventing abuse by landlords, a number of changes should be made. First and foremost, there is no reason why creditors are prohibited from garnisheeing social assistance payments. The current system discourages tenants from acting responsibly, and also lets the social services system off the hook in terms of their responsibility for their clients. The counterargument to this idea is that if creditors were able to collect on these debts, many welfare recipients would be forced into bankruptcy, and their creditors still would not get anything.

This does not seem to us to be a persuasive argument. Personal bankruptcies generally involve individuals who have some assets and for whom the effect of a bankruptcy on their credit rating is a major punishment. These people have an incentive to avoid bankruptcy and as a consequence the per capita bankruptcy rate is low, and the risk to lenders is low. On the other hand, it is true that the incidence of personal bankruptcy would be high among social assistance recipients. Therefore, bankruptcy is not a viable approach to dealing with this situation. The obvious solution is for social services to enforce discipline on clients who default on their responsibilities. The entitlement that clients enjoy should be counterbalanced by penalties for bad actors. Social services should be required to extract fines from clients who have not paid their bills, and should turn the money over to the creditor along with a matching payment from social services. The total payments to the creditor could be capped at two thirds of the money owed, so that all three parties would equally share in the risk and financial loss of client defaults.

The second important reform addresses the ridiculous amount of time that a tenant is legally allowed to remain in her home after she stops paying rent. There is no reason why the landlord should have to wait so long while a succession of seemingly interminable mandatory waiting periods are exhausted. Also, the landlord has to take several actions and pay the Board $150 and the sheriff $325 to get the tenant out. Why should there be such a heavy burden on the landlord, when she is the victim? To better balance the legitimate concerns of landlords and tenants, the eviction process should be streamlined to ensure that a tenant who does not pay her rent can be evicted no later than the middle of the month. The landlord would then, in most cases, be able to repair the place, clean it up and have a chance to re-rent it before the end of the month. This may seem draconian, but the fact is that the tenant will have to move anyway if she doesn't pay. Occupying a rental property is not a sacred right, and the tenant would not be harmed by having to move out promptly. If she is just running short of money, social services should take care of the problem. If it turns out that the landlord has wrongfully evicted the tenant, the tenant should have recourse through the Board, and should be able to seek a suitable penalty against the landlord.

To achieve a two-week maximum waiting period, we suggest that, at the landlord's discretion, the N4 notice can be dispensed with, and the L1 can be issued on the second day of the month. A hearing date should be set for ten days after the L1 is issued. The landlord can call the sheriff and pre-arrange for him to evict the tenant on the eleventh day. The tenant can choose to dispute the L1. If the Board rules in favour of the tenant, the landlord would be required to notify the sheriff not to evict the tenant. This approach discourages unjustified eviction attempts because the landlord has to pay the L1 filing fee and the sheriff's fee. If the landlord were to try to evict his tenant without a solid reason, he would pay a severe price. Because this approach would increase the stakes for both parties, it would put more responsibility on the Board, to ensure that the landlord has a good case, or to ensure that the tenant deserves to stay. The problem with the current system is that in simple cases of nonpayment of rent the tenant always wins and the landlord always loses, no matter what the Board decides.

The third reform is the elimination of start-up fees for welfare recipients who are evicted for non-payment of rent. These start-up fees are totally wrong-headed. They should only be used for tenants who are illegally evicted, i.e. locked out of their home, or for those whose home has become uninhabitable for no fault of their own. Of course, recipients of social assistance are like anyone else in the sense that they may want to move to a nicer place, get better furniture, etc, but why can't they just save to do it rather than count on a handout from social services?

The fourth measure would be to make Board fees proportional to the rent. Currently landlords pay a flat $150 fee to file an application, and tenants pay a flat $45. As a result, landlords of low-income tenants are indirectly subsidizing their tenants. These landlords are generally less able to pay than those who operate more expensive units because the fee represents a much bigger proportion of their income on the unit and because they have to evict their low-income tenants much more frequently. This has the perverse effect of discouraging low-income housing. Why would someone want to own rental property that is discriminated against in this way?

There's no reason why everyone should pay the same fee—the precedent for different fees for different people has already been set, as mentioned above. Tenants currently pay $45 to file an application, whereas landlords pay $150. Presumably tenants are assumed to be less able than landlords to pay for essentially the same service from the Board. Applying the same logic, those landlords who are struggling to provide affordable housing to low income Ontarians should be given a break. We suggest that the landlord's filing fee should be the same as the tenant's fee for the most inexpensive units, say $450 per month and below, and should increase on a sliding scale up to $150 on expensive units, say $1,500 and above. Better yet, why not make the sliding scale apply to both landlord's and tenant's application fees? That seems much fairer to us than simply forcing owners of affordable housing to subsidize everyone else. It may be argued that these landlords use the Board "service" more than others and therefore should pay for it. The answer is that the current system will lead to more conversions of rental property to owner-occupied accommodation, and this will result in an increase in the incidence of homelessness.

The next change would be to allow landlords to collect a cleaning/ damage deposit from a new tenant. Currently, landlords can collect a "security deposit," which legally can be no more than one month's rent. The security deposit is intended to pay for the "last month" of a tenant who stops paying her rent. As we've seen, it is currently impossible to evict a tenant within one month, so this is a partial measure, at best. More importantly, it doesn't cover additional expenses the landlord incurs due to damage or junk left behind by a tenant. Therefore, landlords should also be able to collect a cleaning/damage deposit of up to one month's rent. One may argue that this is open to abuse by the landlord, i.e. she may simply not refund the deposit even if the tenant leaves the unit in pristine condition. Therefore, there should be significant penalties for a landlord who unjustly withholds the deposit. She should be required to give solid evidence of the cleaning/repair costs within a reasonable period of time.

In the *Toronto Star* article we mentioned earlier, Ontario Housing Minister John Gerretsen said he was planning to introduce new tenant protection legislation. That legislation turned out to be the Residential Tenancies Act, and as we've explained above, the new legislation accedes to the demands of tenant groups by extending the time that a tenant can stay in her home before being evicted. This is unconscionable, as it will only increase the ongoing forced transfer of money from landlords to tenants. Ultimately, it will only promote homelessness.

2

A Rude Beginning

Initially, we were very excited about the idea of being landlords and renting out houses. Although we do not live in Windsor, we saw that property values in that city were low relative to the rent that could be charged. We looked at many houses in Windsor that were in our price range. They were older houses, either single-family homes or duplexes. Some were in pretty bad shape, and others were not too bad. We filtered out the bad ones and made our choices. They would need some repairs, but we thought that once they were fixed up they would stay that way and we could look forward to an appreciation in their value. An abundance of tourists were coming from Detroit to gamble at Windsor's new casino. Some weekends when we drove to Windsor, we couldn't find a motel vacancy. We ended up sleeping in the duplexes that we were fixing up, on mattresses that we brought from home. Looking back at it, it was a lot of fun. We were excited. It didn't matter if we didn't get the best night's sleep.

We tried to keep to a budget. We didn't go overboard about how much we were putting into the houses. We tried to find inexpensive carpeting, fixtures, etc., as we knew some tenants could be hard on a place. That was an understatement, as we discovered later. We found a retired gentleman named Willy who was willing to do odd jobs for us, and prospects were looking pretty good.

We put ads in the paper and we had Willy show our properties to prospective tenants. We had decided ahead of time how much our rents would be and whether or not the rent would include utilities. We decided on rent "plus utilities" for one of our properties, a single-family home, and included the utilities in the rent for all the others.

We were all set. Willy went to town showing our properties. The majority of our responses from the ads were from people on social assistance or disability. When we asked if they had last month's rent, they would say that they only had $200 towards last month's rent. We hesitated to take these people as tenants, but when we realized that these were the only kind of calls we were getting we decided to take a chance on them. We'll let you know the outcome in succeeding chapters.

In retrospect, we had problems with tenants right from the beginning. Our very first tenant complained that the upstairs of the detached house was cold and, as a result, she only wanted to pay half the rent. We checked the house and found it was fine. She also complained that her heating bill was too high. She let Charles check her bills and he found that she hadn't paid the bill for three months. She skipped out soon after that. Later, we got a bill from the City of Windsor for unpaid water bills that she was, ostensibly, responsible for. Apparently responsibility, defined as a signed promise by a tenant to pay for something, can easily translate into the landlord's responsibility if the tenant decides she doesn't want to pay. We were surprised and felt that it was disgraceful that the "system" allows tenants to evade their responsibilities just because the landlord is an easy target for a creditor to collect from. This kind of expediency is similar to the "group punishment" used in schools. If a student does something wrong, the teacher punishes the whole class to try to get someone to snitch. In a perverse way, perhaps this is good for the innocent students, who will then go into the world distrustful and assuming that everyone is out to get them. This mindset would be especially useful for anyone planning to become a landlord.

Our next purchase was a duplex with a separate basement unit. All three units were occupied, and each of the tenants had signed an affidavit stating that they had paid last month's rent to the previous owner.

We closed the purchase in December. None of the tenants paid their January rent. One day, we visited the upper unit. The woman who answered the door said that the tenant was busy. We saw a man come out of out of the bedrooms and head down the front stairs. This tenant left at the end of January. We got a private investigator to locate her after she moved to try to collect the rent she owed. The PI told us that she was running an escort service. The tenant in the main floor unit continued to stay and we had to evict her for nonpayment of rent. The tenant in the basement also left at the end of January.

We realized that we were probably the victims of a scam. The previous owner let his deadbeat tenants (who probably weren't paying him rent either) sign the affidavit, meaning that we were legally stuck with giving each of them a rent-free month, funded by the last month's rent that they had supposedly paid, but that we had never received. We learned from this experience, and for our subsequent purchases we demanded in the offer to purchase that the owner pay us the last month's rent for both units, whether or not anyone was living there.

The houses we bought were, with one exception, duplexes. We made sure they were all "retro-fitted" and that we had certificates from the city proving they were up to standard and had passed inspection upon closing. What a joke! Recently, we were slapped with a work order by the fire inspector for a property that passed a fire inspection five years earlier and that was not modified since then. Luckily the required repairs were not extensive. Two steel doors needed to be upgraded and a small area with wood-paneled walls needed to be dry walled for one-hour fire protection. However, the fact is that the wall that originally passed an inspection was never changed or altered by us. It wouldn't make sense for anyone to tear down drywall and replace it with paneling in that area. Either the fire inspector who first inspected the property neglected to see the problem, or made a mistake.

Because of the mistake, we have had to make repairs that the previous owner should have made. We also had to give our tenant a rent abatement because the defect was not originally identified. The fire inspector told us that the fire code has not changed since the original inspection, but refused our request to issue a statement saying that they had made a mistake. The area that needs drywall is a "common" area or laundry room, shared only by the main unit and the upper unit of the house. This room hasn't changed and the use of the room by tenants from both units hasn't changed. While we don't question the need for the repair to meet the fire code, we are asking ourselves: "Did our tax money benefit us by paying the salary of the inspector?" It doesn't look like it.

Although the repair was relatively minor, it still cost us over $4,000. It's worthwhile to note that this cost wouldn't be a problem if our house were in the Toronto area, where a comparable house is worth $500,000. However, in Windsor where the house is worth less than $100,000 and property values are stagnant, or even falling, it's hard to justify spending even $4,000 on repairs. Logic suggests that in this situation many properties in Windsor are being allowed to deteriorate, and will likely have to be condemned within the next five to ten years. We'll have more to say about this in Chapter 8.

3

Case I—The Pimp and I: Brenda

Ah ... Ah ... Ah ... Thumpa ... Thumpa ... Thump ...
Ah ... Ah ... Ah ... Thumpa ... Thumpa ... Thump ...
Ring ... Ring ... Thumpa ... Thumpa ... Thump ... Ah ... Ah ... Ah ... Ring ... Ring ... Ring ...

These were the sounds we could hear as we were working in the basement of one of our rental properties. We had bought the duplex a couple of months previously, and were trying to put up two-by-fours to make a storage room. But it was very hard to concentrate on our work as these sounds were coming from upstairs all morning, accompanied by a phone constantly ringing. After much deliberation, we came to the conclusion that Brenda, our new tenant in the main floor unit, was prostituting herself. This was quite a surprise to us, as we knew she was on social assistance. The sounds we were making as we worked on the storage room, such as hammering and using a power saw, were not making any impression on her as she continued doing what was to her, her job.

As we quickly learned, sex-industry workers are a staple of the rental business in Windsor. After all, Windsor has one of the highest concentrations of strip clubs and massage parlours of any city in Ontario, and the employees of these establishments need to live somewhere. Some of the sex-industry workers carry on their trade in their homes. Based on our own observations and discussions with tenants, information from credit checks, and even private investigator reports, we estimate that 10 percent of our tenants over the years have been hookers, escorts, or Internet porn performers, and another 10 percent have been strippers or "dancers," as they prefer to call themselves.

Later on in the afternoon, while we took a break from our labours, Brenda also seemed to take a break, and met us in the back yard. We took the opportunity to ask her to move her car off the backyard lawn. Downtown Windsor is old, and most properties do not have driveways in front of the house. However, there is an alley behind most properties providing access for vehicles. At Brenda's place, we have a gravel parking area connected to the alley, with parking spots for both units in the duplex. There is a railroad tie separating the parking area from the lawn. For some reason, Brenda had decided to drive, or push, the car off the gravel area, over the railroad tie, and onto the grass. It was springtime, and the car's tires had sunk into the soft ground, making ruts about six inches deep in the lawn.

At first Brenda refused to move the car, as she said it wouldn't start. But when we noticed a tall, smartly dressed, bald man in her presence, Eileen asked if the three of us (Charles, our handyman Willy, and the bald man, who, by the way he was dressed and the bling that he sported, could have been her pimp) could work together to push the car over the railroad tie and onto the gravel. At first, her acquaintance (we'll call him the pimp) snickered, but then he caved in to our request. Eileen enjoyed the comical sight of her husband, our overweight, beer-bellied handyman Willy, and the pimp working together. It could have been a scene from *Seinfeld*.

This is just one of the many situations we have experienced during our ten years of owning rental properties in Windsor. It might seem comical, but it is really quite sad. It was sad what she was doing to herself and her kids, as well as what she was doing to the government and to ordinary citizens through our taxes. We are being screwed!

Brenda was able to rent from us by using a shady ploy. We had done a credit check using the information she supplied in her rental application, and found a few minor balances owing, but nothing serious. Soon after she moved in, we noticed a letter in her mailbox from Windsor social services addressed to Brenda Smith (not her real name), which was a different surname than she had supplied us with. We re-checked her credit rating using the alias along with her other information she had given us, and found a long list of unpaid bills. Normally, the first credit check should have picked up the alias and all of her unpaid debts. It might be interesting to find out why that didn't happen in this case, but we don't have time to investigate all of the irregularities perpetrated by various individuals and organizations. In any case, it was clear that the identity of the individual known by social services as their "client" was different than the mysteriously sanitized identity known to us. It was also clear that she owed an uncollectable fortune to various people, and that Windsor social services was well aware of that, but that they continued to pay their client no matter what (was Windsor social services really unaware that Brenda was a prostitute?).

Brenda failed to pay her rent at the start of her third month in our place, and we followed the procedure prescribed in the Tenant Protection Act (since replaced by the Residential Tenancies Act—see Chapter 1) to evict her. She disputed our application for eviction, and was able to stay in the unit for the third, fourth, and half of the fifth month while the eviction process slowly wound to a conclusion. Although she had paid last month's rent, she had stiffed us for one and a half month's rent plus legal costs, including the $150 application fee to the Ontario Rental Housing Tribunal, and the sheriff's fee of $325, for a total of about $1,500. In addition, we continued to pay for her heat, hydro and water and also supplied free laundry facilities while she continued to live rent-free.

A few weeks after Brenda was evicted, Willy told us that he had seen her plying her trade one night on Wyandotte St. in downtown Windsor.

Brenda is a good example of the landlord's second-worst nightmare: a tenant who pays her rent for a couple of months, then stops paying and drags out the eviction process as much as possible. In Chapter 1, we explained exactly how the landlord-tenant and social welfare systems make it easy for a tenant to live rent-free, at the landlord's expense, for at least two months before moving on. We'll describe a real-life example of the landlord's **worst** nightmare in Chapter 6.

4

Case II—The Wayward Toilet: The Feelgood Family

We first met the Feelgood Family on a cold winter day in 2000, soon after we closed on the purchase of one of our houses. The Feelgood story can be thought of as a kind of low-income version of the *Dynasty* soap opera from the 1980's—the saga of a sprawling, larger-than-life family. It's the story of a family whose lifestyle is as foreign to the average citizen as that of the Colbys and the Carringtons, although the Feelgoods are situated at the opposite pole of the social and economic spectrum from the denizens of *Dynasty*.

The story of the Feelgoods begins at a time before they became our responsibility. The initial phase of the story illustrates the fact that there are any number of inhabitants of downtown Windsor who are not necessarily tenants, but who have a knack for creating headaches nonetheless.

The closing day for the particular house in question was actually pretty complicated. The owner, who we'll call Larry Parks, had been living in the basement when we first went through the house with our realtor. After we had reached an agreement to buy the house, Larry let it be known through his real estate agent that he could be a handyman for us if we let him stay in the basement. We told him that we had our own repairman and that when we made our offer we wanted vacant possession. He had agreed to the vacant possession stipulation as part of the agreement of purchase and sale, so everything seemed set. On the day of closing Eileen suspected that Larry could still be living in the basement and called our realtor to go to the house and check it out. We made it clear that if he were still there, we would not be closing. Sure enough, he was there! Our realtor had to tell him that unless he moved out that day we would not close the deal—ever. He did move out, but only a few steps to the house next door, which he also owned. We've had to put up with him all these years; he's apparently held quite a bit of resentment towards us even though we were not at fault, and has not been the kind of neighbour one would hope for.

If we had closed the deal without ensuring that Larry had vacated, it's clear that he would have become our tenant, with all of the rights attendant to residential tenancy in Ontario. If he declined to pay any rent, we might have been able to apply to the Tribunal to evict him. However, since we had no rental agreement, and particularly no agreement on the monthly rent, he probably could have used that to stall the eviction for many months, and never have to pay a penny. He would have claimed that, in spite of the vacant possession clause in the agreement of purchase and sale, we verbally agreed to let him stay for a nominal rent in return for handyman services.

The trap here is that if we admitted to the Tribunal adjudicator that we had received an offer from him to that effect, the adjudicator would assume that a negotiation had gone on, and then the burden of proof that we had turned down the offer of handyman services would rest with us. After all, the if the agreement of purchase and sale stipulated vacant possession, but we had not ensured that the house was vacant on closing, it's very likely that we had a verbal agreement that Larry could stay (in the mind of a pro-tenant adjudicator). And if we didn't want him to stay, but hadn't checked that he was gone before closing, that's our own damn fault! This is downtown Windsor after all—you don't just take someone at his word that he will be out, even if you have a signed contract.

What would it have taken to evict Larry? The adjudicator would have ruled that he could stay, subject to paying reasonable rent in return for handyman services. It's not likely that the adjudicator would have imposed an agreement between us, but if we didn't come to an agreement with Larry we would still have to apply again to evict him, there would be a hearing, and he would simply argue that we refused to come to an agreement and live up to our end of the bargain. In other words, there would be no way to evict him, nor to collect any rent from him.

The other aside to this story is that we also agreed to purchase another house just down the street at about the same time. This particular house needed quite a few repairs, but the price was good. All went well until a few days before the closing date. We got a phone call from our lawyer, who had found an irregularity on the vendor's side while performing the title search. Apparently, the person who signed the agreement of purchase and sale was not the owner of the house, but was actually the owner's husband. It seems that he had been representing himself as the owner to his own realtor. This may not seem to be particularly important, but in this case the husband had actually transferred ownership of the house to his wife a few months earlier. The wife was not living in Canada, and our lawyer discovered that the husband had been charged by Revenue Canada with evading $50,000 in GST owing from operating a convenience store.

If we had followed through with the purchase, Revenue Canada would very likely have been able to put a $50,000 lien on the property. Most likely, the husband would have been able to offload his tax problem onto us, or at least saddle us with an expensive and time-consuming legal problem. Of course, we did not close the deal, and consider ourselves lucky to have escaped from a disaster. The scary thing is that our lawyer discovered the problem essentially by chance. Any existing lien on the property would have been easily discovered, but it is much more difficult to protect against the delayed consequences of nefarious behaviour.

The moral of these stories is "expect anyone you don't know well to try to screw you, especially someone from downtown Windsor."

Anyway … getting back to the Feelgoods. After the closing of our purchase, we took a look at the property. The house was vacant except for the upper unit. As we began to ascend the stairs, low and behold, the members of not just one family, but two families met us. There were a total of thirteen people crowded into a two bedroom upper unit, like the proverbial sardines. A nest of mice might be a better analogy. We couldn't believe our eyes. Mama Mae and her lesbian partner Sally had five kids crammed into an unheated attic closet off one of the bedrooms. Mama Mae had an electric heater keeping them warm. The closet or storage area was big enough to hold two sets of bunk beds and another bed. The other family included Mama Mae's sister Susie Sweetcheeks and her boyfriend Arnold, along with their four kids. Susie Sweetcheeks said that the owner had promised her the main floor unit in the same house. We had already promised the main unit to another applicant so we had to come up with a solution. We could have called the health department for overcrowding, but decided to offer them another house that was bigger. We let Susie's family stay, and moved Mama Mae's crowd to a three-bedroom main floor unit. That seemed to have satisfied them.

As an aside, the agreement of purchase and sale required the previous owner to seek our agreement if he wished to rent a unit to a new tenant before closing the sale. The Feelgoods definitely weren't living there when we first viewed the house.

After we moved Mama Mae's family to their own unit, we noticed that there were always loads of people there. Mama Mae said she had a big family (six brothers and sisters) and they were always visiting. However, many of the people seemed to be coming and going, and there were always people we didn't recognize. It was actually quite depressing seeing our house overrun by people, most of whom didn't seem very nice, to put it mildly. Mama Mae acquired a large attack dog that barked and snarled at us, jumping up against the front door when we would knock on the door, and it had to be restrained if we had to enter the premises for some reason. Often, there was another attack dog visiting. We quickly began to suspect some potentially illegal "goings on" from Mama Mae and her crowd. Eileen sat in the car one day as Charles worked on the house. She noticed that there were a lot of young adults coming and going—staying for five minutes and leaving. We thought our suspicions were right, but what could we do? We had called the police in the past and they did absolutely nothing.

Meanwhile, back at the other house Mama Mae's sister Susie Sweetcheeks and her family quickly got themselves into our bad books. They were often late paying their rent, but that wasn't our main concern. Whenever we visited them, Susie and Arnold were spaced out, beyond what we would expect if they were just smoking dope. Worse still, their children appeared to be neglected. Their youngest, a little girl who was no more than a toddler, looked unkempt, with dirty, tangled hair. We remember seeing the little girl standing at the top of the stairs where she could easily have been bumped over the edge by one of her siblings or even the "adults" in their altered state of consciousness. Her mother was there, but didn't recognize the potential danger. We learned quickly that all of the enforcement of building and fire codes in the world doesn't help much if people aren't aware of basic safety. In the end, the health care system and the public has to pick up the pieces.

After a few months we hinted to Susie, not too diplomatically, that we knew what she was doing and that it would be best if the family moved out. They did leave within a few days, and they were out of our hair, although we did see Susie occasionally at Mama Mae's place. Soon afterward, we learned that the children had been taken away from Susie by children's aid. Although this was an unpleasant, if not tragic development, we felt a sense of relief that they had left our property before something serious happened to them, or us. This may seem heartless, but we are landlords, not social workers, health care workers, or police officers. At times, it feels as though we are expected to take on those responsibilities, but that expectation is unrealistic, and is part of the reason why the system is so dysfunctional.

After about two years, Mama Mae asked if her sister Lulu could move into the vacant upper unit above her. We reluctantly said yes. Mama Mae had always paid her rent even though her crowd was rough on the property. She even had friends repair a few things.

Lulu seemed a little ditzy, but we learned to put up with her until the day of the fire. Mama Mae called us one evening at dinnertime and said there was a fire in the upper unit. She told us the fire department had it under control. When we asked one of the firefighters on site what had happened, he told us the fire had started from careless cooking. Lulu had left a pot on the stove with her boyfriend asleep on the couch and went downstairs to visit Mama Mae. The greasy contents of the pot had caught fire and … voila!

Luckily, no one was hurt and the damage wasn't catastrophic, although the fire department estimated it at $5,000. The drywall behind the stove was damaged, and the stove and fridge were totaled. The ceilings and walls in the kitchen, and adjoining hallway were blackened, but only within a foot or two of the top. The carpets in the hallway and on the stairs were soggy, dark, and smoky-smelling from the water used to put out the fire.

We had another fridge and stove stored in a basement so we moved them over to Lulu's place, and cleaned and repainted the kitchen and hallway. We never charged Lulu for moving the appliances over, or for the replacement costs, or the cleaning costs. We certainly didn't file a claim with our insurance company. That would have cost us more than what we could have claimed.

The final straw came when Lulu complained that her toilet was not working. We sent our repairman Willy to investigate. He decided that we needed a new toilet and got a used one from Habitat. He delivered it and set it in the kitchen temporarily. He told Lulu he would install it the next day. When he returned the following day, he found that Lulu and her brood had been using the new toilet, although it wasn't even installed yet and was just sitting on the kitchen floor. She was also dumping it in the sink. The fact is that there was no need for Lulu to do this as she could easily use her sister Mama Mae's facilities. Willy couldn't get over it and to this day talks about it with disgust.

All in all, Mama Mae lasted about four years with us, but eventually she failed to pay her rent one month. Her sister Lulu and her mother, who lived in one of our other houses, also failed to pay their rent. Mama Mae claimed that her rent money, as well as Lulu's, had been stolen from her bedroom. However, given the fact that all three relatives stopped paying at the same time, it seems obvious to us that something happened that affected all of the Feelgoods at that time. It may be coincidental, but there had been a major drug bust in the city and it occurred to us that it might have had a ripple effect on the Feelgoods. In any case, we had to evict all three branches of the Feelgood family, at great expense to ourselves. We received no rent for Mama Mae's unit for six months, taking into account the time taken to evict her plus the time needed to repair the place. Lulu's unit was out of service for five months. Our poor house has never been able to get completely back on its feet. We suspect it was widely known in downtown Windsor as a "crack house" before we bought it, and a succession of tenants that have subsequently rented the place have done nothing to allay that suspicion.

Soon after the Feelgoods were evicted, we heard that children's aid took away both Mama Mae's children and Lulu's children.

There are certain details in the Feelgood story that are common threads running through the stories of many of our tenants. The first is the "someone stole my rent money" excuse for not paying rent. We get this surprisingly often, and we invariably receive no more rent from the tenant in question, ever. It's as though their source of funds has permanently dried up. When asked, these tenants always say they've filed a police report, but this is dubious. In any case, our experience is that the police are "o-for" in solving these "crimes."

By the way, it's difficult to get a copy of a police report, even if it involves a crime against our property, because a request has to be filed under the Access to Information Act. As an aside, the difficulties we've experienced getting police action to deal with illegal activity by tenants reminds us of an incident Charles observed at a local supermarket recently. A security guard took down a young woman in one of the shopping aisles. Within minutes, there were three police cruisers in front of the store to complete the arrest. Apparently, she had snuck some food out of the store without paying. Now, we're sure she couldn't have taken more than $100 worth of food, but the cost of that police operation to protect the property of that supermarket must have been several times that much, duly paid for by ordinary taxpayers. On the other hand, if $700 were really to be stolen from one of our tenants, or from us for that matter, we doubt that the police would do anything about it.

An important theme running through many of our stories, including the story of the Feelgoods, is what we call the "marijuana economy." This concept is easiest to grasp by first realizing that low-income people don't participate in the conventional economy to the same degree as middle class Ontarians. However, taking up the slack is a second, underground economy which most of them are involved in to some degree. Some of our tenants have seemed to be more involved in the marijuana economy than the conventional economy. Marijuana is much more than just a drug, and even more than a source of income. It is a kind of currency, and there is a kind of "marijuana society" founded on it, much as conventional middle class society revolves around money (and golf).

Interestingly, we have never found evidence of any significant grow operations in any of our units—no unexplained high or low hydro bills (we pay for the utilities), no windows blocked off. However, there have been many tenants who seemed to have visitors in and out all day and night.

If you belong to the marijuana economy, one of the prerequisites is an attack dog. The reason is obvious: an attack dog is a legal weapon that can be used to intimidate or even assault an enemy without fear of any significant consequences from the police or legal system. Most of our tenants have owned dogs, and without exception they have all been attack dogs. Actually, one of our tenants had a small dog, but she got rid of it within a couple of months and replaced it with a Doberman. Pit bulls are the pet of choice, but with the severe restrictions that have been placed on pit bulls throughout Ontario recently, it remains to be seen how they will fare. We always ask prospective tenants if they have a dog, and ninety percent of the time they say no. Sometimes, they tell the truth but still try to pull the wool over our eyes. A favourite ploy is to refer to the dog as a Staffordshire Terrier, as if we don't know that it's a variation on the pit bull. You can be sure that a Staffordshire Terrier bears no similarity to a Yorkshire Terrier, although that's obviously what the caller is hoping we'll think, in order to get a foot in the door. Another breed that crops up occasionally is the Cane Corso. We googled it, and found out that it's an Italian attack dog.

We're not sure how much of the attack dog craze is a real need for protection and how much is fad or fashion. Given that absolutely none of our pet-loving tenants have owned anything smaller than a pit bull, it's easy to conclude that owning a small dog is definitely uncool in the marijuana economy. If the crackdown on pit bulls takes away weapons from certain people, they will likely turn to other weapons. For the time being, there is one thing each of our attack-dog-owning tenants will say if asked: their pet is just a gentle softie.

5

Case III—The Digger: Pamela and Bobby

This is one for the books!

We rented a one-bedroom apartment to a nice looking girl, who we'll call Pamela. When we showed the unit to her and her boyfriend Bobby, she appeared to be very sweet and innocent. We could see that she was very young, and we discovered from her credit report that she had just turned seventeen. She paid last month's rent up front, and everything checked out on her credit check. She moved in on December first.

The next week, on visiting the property we noticed a big piece of machinery parked on a trailer in Pamela's parking spot in the back of the property. We knocked on her door to ask her about it but there was no answer. We were very concerned about the "digger," as we called it. It looked very dangerous and there were small children living in the neighborhood who might be injured if they were tempted to climb onto the machine. We tried calling the phone number that she had given us, but there was no answer. We left a note in her mailbox, asking her to call us.

Because Pamela didn't contact us, we contacted our paralegal and she suggested we leave a 48-hour notice in Pamela's mailbox, requiring her to move the "digger," or we would have it towed. She explained that having given the notice, we would be legally entitled to remove it from our property. We delivered the notice, and expected that Pamela would do the logical thing and remove the digger, or at least call us to complain about the notice. However, there was still no response from Pamela, so ... we had the digger towed. That finally provoked a response, but not from Pamela—it was from the police. A police officer called and said that someone named Bobby was accusing us of stealing his digger. We told the cop that our paralegal had put up a 48-hour notice for them to remove the digger, and that since Pamela didn't remove it, we had the right to have it towed. We also asked why Bobby had complained. The cop said he was the tenant at the property. We said we didn't rent our apartment to a Bobby—that the official tenant was Pamela and as far as we knew she was the sole occupant of the unit. We told him our paralegal would call the police to confirm that she had posted the 48-hour notice for us. We pointed out to the police officer that we were concerned about the risk that the digger posed for the children in the area, but he didn't seem the least bit concerned about the danger.

Our paralegal informed the police where Pamela and Bobby could find the digger. We even got a call from Bobby's employer, threatening us with legal action and vehemently insisting that we couldn't get away with this. When Pamela and Bobby came to pick up the digger, we had them sign a statement promising not to return the digger to our property. That evening, our repairman Willy phoned us and asked us to guess what was in our backyard again. We had to issue another 48-hour notice. Do you think we had it towed again? You guessed it. This time the police didn't call. Pamela and Bobby asked where they could pick it up. We told them it was way out of town and advised them not to bring it back to our property.

Pamela didn't pay her January rent on time, so we issued her a notice to start the eviction process. She didn't seem to have a phone, so one day in early January we stopped by to see if she was planning to pay the rent. A young woman we had never met answered the door. We could see several young men through the open door. The young woman said that Pamela wasn't there, so we asked her to ask Pamela to call us.

A few days later, the tenant in the upper unit called to say that she could smell marijuana smoke from Pamela's unit coming up through the ventilation system. The police visited the place and observed the occupants of Pamela's place smoking dope. They just told them to stop doing it. The partying continued and we lost the tenant living in the upper unit, as she claimed that she couldn't stand the smell.

After the sheriff evicted the occupants of Pamela's unit, we changed the locks. The sheriff posted a 48-hour notice on the door for Pamela to remove the furniture and other personal belongings. No one contacted us to get the furniture, but we needed to clean and repair the place so it could be re-rented, so we took it out of the unit and left it in the back yard. We found a bong and some hydroponics equipment, but no evidence of a significant drug operation. The following evening, our repairman was doing some repairs in the unit and some of the evicted occupants came back. Because the locks were changed, they couldn't get in, so they kicked in a window. Our repairman Willy called 911. The police arrived quickly and had an altercation with the thugs, one of whom actually assaulted one of the policemen. There was a chase on foot, the bad guys were caught, and they were thrown in jail. They had left the place in a mess and had actually kicked in the side of the stove.

For anyone who is thinking of becoming a landlord, the moral of this story is: be wary of very young tenants, no matter how well they present themselves, how glowing their references are, or how good their credit report is. For one thing, they don't have a track record as tenants, so there isn't as much information to evaluate them with. A very young person has likely just left home, and likely doesn't have much experience following rules. A young woman, no matter how nice she may appear, almost certainly has a boyfriend, who may be in it for whatever he can get. Like Pamela, she may just be a front for a gang of thugs looking for a cheap place to party.

Another point to consider is that as a landlord, you have to get used to dealing with freeloaders. Pamela and her friends are a perfect example. These people have a deeply ingrained sense of entitlement: where it comes from we have no idea. The attitude is: you don't want me to park my digger on your property, just make me take it away! If you do anything, I'll sue. Just try to get me to stop smoking marijuana—I don't give a shit if it bothers someone with little kids. You don't like my pit bull—too bad.

When you consider that there are hundreds if not thousands of people like this living in downtown Windsor, and realize that each and every one of them probably gets into a situation every day where they have an opportunity to assert their rights, the consequences are mind-boggling. It's amazing that they haven't already all killed each other off.

6

Case IV—The Eve of Destruction: The Failure of the Children's Aid Society

It was about 7 p.m. on a beautiful summer evening as we pulled our 1993 Ford Aerostar into the driveway of one of our properties in Windsor. One of our tenants named Carol had complained about a leaking toilet and we wanted to check it out. It had been about six months since we had been inside her unit, although various repair people had visited the place during that time. Little could we imagine what would occur in the short space of the next half-hour.

Carol had been a tenant of ours for about two years. Our first impression of her was that that she was very nice, but a bit flighty. She was a client of social services and had three children, aged 8, 6 and 3. She admitted, without prompting, that each child had a different father. Social services wanted her to get a job but Carol was worried about her middle child, Andrew, or Andy for short. Andy seemed to be hyperactive and always got into Charles's tools whenever we were working at her house. He would jump onto the back of our van without asking permission.

Little by little, we noticed that damage was being done to the house. Drywall was being damaged. Cover plates for the electrical outlets and switches were missing. Andy admitted to Charles that he unscrewed the cover plates, and Carol admitted that Andy liked to dig at the drywall. Charles reprimanded both Carol and Andy, saying Carol should be watching Andy more closely and telling him no. Charles repaired the drywall and replaced the cover plates.

With each visit, we noticed that the damage was getting worse. Small two-inch holes in the drywall were now four inches in diameter. One wall in the back bedroom was completely destroyed and bits of plaster covered the carpet. Plaster dust was ground into the carpet. Luckily, the wall was only about four feet wide as it was next to a closet. Charles repaired the wall and the other holes (with the song *Fixing a Hole* from *Sergeant Pepper* continuously running through his mind) and replaced all of the cover plates, but with each succeeding visit the holes were back and cover plates were missing.

To get Andy to behave better, we promised to give him a pack of gum on our next visit if there was no further damage. This seemed to help, so we continued to do it for a few weeks. We felt sorry for Carol and her children, so we would allow her to catch up on her rent when she fell behind, without filing an application for eviction with the Ontario Rental Housing Tribunal (we've described the role of the Tribunal and the detailed eviction process in Chapter 1). One month she failed to pay any rent so we let her use her last month's rent deposit to catch up. Eventually, Carol seemed to be on the right track except for the damage. The living room carpet grew dirtier and dirtier with mud tracked in from outside, until we noticed on one visit that the carpet had been removed, leaving the worn, dirty hardwood strip floor behind. We also noticed four broken windows that Carol said were broken by Andy. Carol said that she would have her boyfriend repair the windows, and he did repair two of the four broken ones. Carol also got a pit bull.

We felt that, to a certain extent, it wasn't Carol's fault if Andy was a behavioural problem. On the other hand, Carol had a friend in the upper unit who also had small children and was receiving social assistance. We suspected that drugs were passing between Carol and her friend, and that Carol's children, especially, were not being properly watched or cared for.

Carol liked to keep her unit hot year-round. In the dead of winter we saw both Andy and Carol's boyfriend du jour walking around shirtless. It's a stereotype, but it reminded us of the bad guys on *Cops* who are invariably shirtless when the cops bust into their place to apprehend them.

We got a call from a children's aid worker asking us if we would give Carol some paint to paint the walls. We told the worker that the place had been painted a year and a half earlier, before Carol moved in, and we would only give her paint if the other two windows were fixed and if she got rid of the pit bull. The worker gave her a deadline to fix the windows and get rid of the dog. She got rid of the dog, but the windows were not fixed. We also asked the CAS worker if they would be monitoring the situation, and she said they would.

Six months later, on that fateful summer evening, we knocked on the front door of Carol's unit. On entering the place, we immediately noticed that she had put sheets over the front bedroom windows and the blinds in the living room were broken.

As part of the repairs and cleaning we do before renting out a unit, we always ensure that there are blinds on every window in the unit. This makes the unit more attractive to prospective tenants and prevents anyone outside the house from seeing in. If blinds are damaged, we replace them with new blinds, since it's usually not worthwhile to repair them. We use the cheapest mini blinds, which are quite presentable and functional.

The fact is that if there were no window coverings most low-income tenants would leave the windows open to view, or put sheets over the windows. Most would certainly not pay for blinds or curtains. In all too many cases, tenants destroy the perfectly usable blinds that we supply. The tenants, their kids, or their dogs break them carelessly. It's as though they prefer to live in squalor, and damage blinds, carpets, moldings, etc, accidentally on purpose.

The holes in the walls, which had been repaired the last time we were there, were back and much bigger than before. Like a cancerous tumour, which metastasizes to various sites around the body, the holes were growing and developing all over the house. One hole about two feet across in the living room extended through the wall to the adjoining bedroom. The dining room hosted at least ten holes of varying sizes, as did the back bedroom. Many of the walls looked as though human excrement had been thrown at them or rubbed on them.

Many of the holes were around electrical outlets and light switches, exposing electrical wiring. The carpets had been removed from two of the bedrooms as well as the living room. Carol had acquired an adult dog as a replacement for the pit bull, and also had large puppy. We told Carol that the damage amounted to at least $2,000 and it had to be fixed. She said that if we would allow her time, she would begin the repairs herself and gradually get them done.

We didn't even have a chance to raise the issue of the carpets, when the puppy let loose what seemed like a gallon of urine on the hardwood floor right in front of us. We couldn't believe our eyes, and Charles turned to Carol and demanded, "What the hell is that?" When Eileen asked Carol if she was going to clean it up, she said, "When I get around to it." That was the straw that broke the camel's back. We had been willing to see if she would repair the drywall, but after seeing her attitude about cleaning up the dog's urine we had had it. We told her that we would serve her an N5 notice in the morning requiring that the damage be repaired in seven days or we would apply to the Tribunal to have her evicted. Then we walked out.

After thinking about the situation for a couple of days, we realized that we couldn't afford to let Carol stay any longer because much more damage was likely to occur. It was five days before the first of the month, and we asked her to use her rent money to find another place and be gone by then. We received a phone call from a children's aid worker saying we couldn't ask her to leave with only five days to find another home. Eileen asked the worker if he had seen the place. He said that he had seen pictures and was planning to make it his "little project to fix it up with Carol." Eileen said, "Little project! You've got to be kidding." Eileen asked to talk to the other caseworker that we had dealt with previously—we'll call her Martha.

Eileen asked Martha if she had been to the house lately. Martha admitted she had had surgery and hadn't visited the place in six months. Eileen said that when they said they would be monitoring the situation, we couldn't believe that they could allow this to happen. We explained about the holes around switches and how big the holes were. Carol was paid a visit by children's aid that night and all three of her kids were taken away. It was sad to see this happen, but we're hoping that the kids might be monitored much more closely by their new family as well as by the children's aid worker.

After visiting our place after Carol left we were able to open the fridge. It was caked with a brownie-like substance. We've heard people bake brownies and add marijuana to them. We were able to open the cupboards, and couldn't believe the jumble of beer and liquor bottles thrown haphazardly behind the cupboard doors. We opened the bathroom door and found the shower curtain rod bent out of shape, as though Andy had been hanging from it. A section of linoleum had been ripped from the bathroom floor.

We've talked to Carol since she moved out and reassured her we didn't call CAS. Carol said she's getting her life together and she's hoping to get her kids back. This is only one case; we have many more. Our whole purpose in writing this book is to bring to the public's attention the fact that our tax money is not being used effectively. We are disillusioned about the welfare system and how it has affected our rental business. We don't know whether this happened because we bought our properties in the city of Windsor or whether it's happening all over the country. Windsor's economy has been going downhill and the border crossing is affecting the city as well (we describe the situation in detail in Chapter 8), so the system may be under greater pressure there than in other municipalities.

Over one year after the "eve of destruction" occurred, a report by Ontario Auditor General Jim McCarter was released that slammed abuses occurring at children's aid societies in the four municipalities that were investigated. The story made front-page news for several days throughout Ontario. According to an article published in the *Toronto Star* on December 6, 2006, abuses were discovered at the Thunder Bay, Toronto, York and Peel CAS. Egregious examples of lavish spending by the CAS units that benefited CAS staff were uncovered, but undoubtedly the most serious issue was the lack of timely action by CAS staff to respond to known threats to children in their homes.

Key findings that were reported in the *Toronto Star* include:

- In 73 percent of cases, comprehensive risk assessments were not completed on time—every 180 days. At one society, the last full assessment was done almost two years prior to the auditor's visit.

- In one-third of the files reviewed, children were not seen within the required twelve hours or seven days—the time limits for children deemed at greatest risk of abuse. Caseworker visits were an average of three weeks late, with one being 165 days late.

- The requirement to visit a child in care every 90 days was not met in 60 percent of the cases reviewed.

- Over the last five years, CAS caseload jumped to 32,785 from 24,806, a 34 percent increase.

Although the Windsor CAS was not audited, there is no doubt in our minds that the problems cited by the auditor in other cities have occurred to at least as great an extent in the Windsor CAS. As we detail throughout this book, there is a culture of entitlement that permeates not just CAS but all of the social services agencies. This practically guarantees that widespread abuses will occur, at least as long as they are permitted to do so by their political masters. Under the circumstances, why would they not occur?

The Liberal government of Ontario has vowed to take action throughout the CAS system to address the problems identified by the auditor. However, we do not have much faith that any reforms, however ineffectual, will extend to other social service agencies. We have not seen any discussion in the news media of the potential for irregularities at social services. As far as we can tell, no one has any inkling that anything could be wrong. It's frustrating to realize that the news media are not doing their job in unearthing abuses at social services, particularly since it is evident to us that this is low-hanging fruit. After the CAS audit findings hit the papers, we contacted the *Toronto Star*, *Globe and Mail*, and the *National Post*, trying to interest them in an investigation of social services. No one from any of these highly regarded papers would talk to us about it.

We are not suggesting that individual cases or names should be revealed as part of an investigation, although it could be argued that doing so would have a salutary effect. What is needed is an understanding of what are the rules, how much discretion is allowed within the rules, how it is ensured that the rules are followed, and how it is demonstrated that they are being followed.

The lack of oversight of social services begs the question: why does the government want the people to be taking advantage of it? It boggles our minds. It's as though the government takes no pride in the welfare system. In reality, it's a joke.

We would really like children's aid and social services to be responsible for the tenants who do not show any responsibility for damaging doors, carpets, appliances, etc. Social services readily gives out a start-up cheque when a tenant has been evicted. We never get a call to enquire why a tenant has been evicted. If social services or children's aid had to pay for damages and rent arrears, then they would have to go after the tenant for what is owed them and it would be interesting to see how they like it.

There's a lot of pressure on landlords to take tenants on social services or disability, but there's no pressure to make these tenants accountable for what they do.

Carol's story illustrates the problem of damage done to rental units by low-income tenants. A similar problem that is less severe but more widespread is the many tenants who do not take proper care of their garbage—Carol was no exception. There is a terrible rat problem in downtown Windsor. It's not unusual to see the bodies of dead rats lying bloated in back alleys, or flattened in the street. The tenants' garbage, if not taken care of in the right way, adds to the problem. Our rental agreements stipulate that tenants have to dispose of their garbage and provide rubber containers for themselves, which they never do. They put out their garbage in black plastic bags, or even grocery bags, days before the designated garbage pick-up. Sure enough, the garbage bags are torn apart by rodents or cats or dogs and the garbage is sprawled across the backyard or alley. Do they go out to pick up the mess? In their way of thinking, this would be beneath them. They wait until we, the landlord, get an eyeful. In one instance an inspector called us and said it was our responsibility to clean up the mess, left behind by a tenant. When we mentioned to him that all of our tenants sign an agreement saying they will dispose of their garbage and that they will provide containers for the garbage, he asked us to fax him a copy. As far as we were concerned this inspector did his job, as the tenant was fined. This is not always the way it turns out. Inspectors call about mattresses, furniture, etc, left out in backyards and alleys by tenants, and then they say it's the landlord's responsibility to get rid of it. Again, they're not making the tenants accountable for the actions—and the tenants still get their welfare cheques.

Damage to the drywall in the front hall closet.

Damaged window with shoddy repair by Carol's boyfriend.

Makeshift window coverings in Carol's front bedroom.

Destroyed blinds in Carol's living room.

Large hole in the wall around a heating duct in the living room. The hole extends through the wall into the adjoining bedroom.

Large holes in the dining room wall. The wall is smeared with filth.

Hole in a bedroom wall, exposing electrical cables.

Multiple holes in a bedroom wall.

Multiple holes in a bedroom wall.

Holes in a bedroom wall near a broken window.

Refrigerator strewn with filth.

Filthy kitchen cabinet littered with beer and liquor bottles.

Junk and filth in a kitchen cabinet.

Filthy kitchen cabinet with beer bottles. Cupboards were damaged, and ceramic tiles were stripped from the counter top. Knobs were removed from the cabinet drawers.

Bent shower curtain rod in the bathroom.

Patch of linoleum ripped from bathroom floor.

Huge hole in the dining room wall. Note the missing electrical plate for the wall switch.

Bedroom door ripped from its hinges. It was obvious that Carol had done nothing to prevent her children from drawing on the walls and doors with crayons, or from doing more serious damage. Carol had ripped out the bedroom carpet, leaving a bare wooden floor.

Debris in the stairwell at the rear exit from Carol's unit.

Garbage and debris in the back yard after Carol vacated.

Garbage and debris at the back entrance to Carol's unit.

Garbage at the back door.

7

Case V—My Pit Bull's Just a Softie: The Fowlers

One of our tenants had been living in an upper unit for about three years. She had been in the duplex when we had purchased it, and had been a good tenant. We'll call her Natalie. The unit below her had become vacant, so we had to try to find another tenant. One man who had seen it (we'll call him Bill) just loved it. He was on disability and asked if he could have a roommate. We asked the prospective room-mate to fill out an application, and we checked her out. Her name was Mary Fowler. Everything seemed fine. Bill would be the official tenant.

A few months had passed when, one day, Mary called and said that Bill was in jail. She said she would like to become the official tenant. It was a complete surprise to us that Bill could be in jail and we told her that we would have to get a written note from him saying that he didn't want to be a tenant of ours anymore. She said she would visit the jail and get a note from him, but time passed and she never got around to collecting the note from Bill. We asked our paralegal to visit him in jail and get the note for us, not particularly to help Mary but mainly out of curiosity. Our paralegal visited the jail and she met Bill, but he claimed that he didn't know anything about the apartment. Bill also claimed that his wallet had been stolen while he was at a party. Our paralegal asked us to describe the Bill that we knew and he didn't fit the description of the guy that our paralegal had visited in jail.

We realized that Bill was likely a victim of identity theft. Presum-ably, our tenant "Bill" had stolen the real Bill's identity. He may have taken off when he found out that the police were after the real Bill, knowing that they might discover his theft of Bill's identity. When we asked Mary about this she claimed that this was a complete surprise to her, and that she hadn't known the "so-called Bill" very long and didn't realize he wasn't who he said he was. We didn't believe her, although it might have been possible that the fake Bill had taken off and then phoned her to say he was in jail. It seemed more likely to us that when she told us that Bill was in jail, she didn't expect us to follow up by visiting him there.

Mary said that she couldn't afford the rent on her own, but said her brother Tim would like to move in with her. He was also on disability. While the best option for us, given our doubts about Mary's veracity, would have been to evict Mary on the grounds that she wasn't our official tenant, it was unlikely that the Tribunal would rule in our favour. So the Fowlers, brother and sister, became our tenants.

Natalie called us one day and asked us if we knew that the Fowlers had two pit bulls. We told her that we weren't aware of it. She said that Tim always had them chained up on the front porch and she was scared to death to go in and out the front door.

We phoned Mary and asked about the dogs, but she denied having the dogs tied up on the porch and said that they only had one dog. Natalie called the next day and said she had taken her dining room chairs out onto the front lawn to clean them, and Tim had poured beer all over them. He had also used the garden hose to shoot water into her living room through her front window. We questioned the Fowlers and of course they denied it. We visited the house and found two pit bulls in the backyard. When Tim saw that Eileen had been looking in the backyard he gave her the finger.

We called the City about the dogs and they said they would pay the Fowlers a visit. Things started escalating. Before long we got a phone call from Natalie saying that there were police knocking on the Fowlers' door. Mary had actually called them, as Tim had locked her out. Tim would not open the door to the police. The whole time the police were there, Natalie was on the phone with Eileen and Eileen could hear the shouting on the phone. In the end, Tim took off and Mary was left alone, again. Mary gave us a written notice stating that she would be out by the end of the month (we waived the usual sixty days notice requirement just to get rid of her), but when she didn't leave as promised, we started to put her furniture outside the unit. She showed up with the police and we had to put her stuff back in. Happily, within a couple of weeks she notified us that she was gone.

A major problem that we have, as a landlord, is that we cannot tell a tenant she cannot have a dog or cat. The newspaper ad can say "no pets" to help filter out people with dogs, but legally we cannot veto pets. A tenant might not have a dog when she moves in, but we cannot stop her from getting a dog after she moves in. It has been the trend recently for tenants to get attack dogs, not only for protection, but also to deter the landlords to visit.

8

Windsor 911

We recently came across something that neatly encapsulates the challenge that Windsor faces. Harvard University economist Edward Glasser is quoted in an April 11, 2007 *Toronto Star* article on decaying American cities as saying that Detroit has "no economic or geographic reason" to exist. He views the prospects for any rebound in the city, hit hard by the declining auto industry, as dim. We believe that the statement would be equally valid with "Detroit" replaced by "Windsor."

In Chapter 1, we discussed some information about the Ontario welfare and landlord-tenant system, which is salient to the landlord-tenant relationship. We've made the case that local and provincial governments have conspired to transfer money from landlords to tenants via the welfare and landlord-tenant system. We've also provided, in previous chapters and in the chapters to come, many true stories that reflect the widespread abusive behaviour by low-income tenants towards their landlords in Windsor. There is no doubt in our minds that the poor economic condition of the city of Windsor has exacerbated the abuses that are encouraged by the system. How bad is the situation in Windsor and how did Windsor arrive at its current sorry condition?

The difficulty of the situation in Windsor is easily gauged by a visit to the city, or by even an occasional reader of the *Windsor Star*. Hardly a day goes by without some new disaster befalling the city, or the threat of a catastrophe just around the corner. Each new revelation is accompanied by much lamentation and hand wringing on the part of *Star* editors, columnists, guest experts, and letter writers. We'll expand on this later in this chapter, but suffice it to say that, in spite of the ready availability of this news and information, a full appreciation of the decaying condition of the city can only be had by being there, on the streets and, as we so often are, in the households of downtown Windsor's low-income citizens. We'll begin with a review of the events that have made Windsor what it is today.

Windsor has always been a blue-collar town. The economy is dominated first and foremost by the auto industry and to a lesser extent by the distillery business. The story of the emergence of nearby Detroit as the focus of the US auto industry early in the twentieth century has been told many times. In suburban Dearborn Michigan in 1908, Henry Ford invented the Model T Ford. In 1913 he began to manufacture the Model T using an assembly line, and thereby revolutionized the manufacturing process. Thousands of southerners, both white and African American streamed north to take advantage of employment opportunities in the factories of Ford and other auto pioneers. Detroit boomed. The 1916 census showed that the city's population of 571,784 had grown by 17% since 1910. In 1917, Detroit was described as "one of the most beautiful cities in the Union."

Lying just across the Detroit River from Detroit was its Canadian suburb, Windsor. All of the major auto manufacturers established plants in Windsor, and the city shared in the prosperity of its American parent. The area surrounding the Ford plant in the eastern outskirts of Windsor was dubbed Ford city.

When Prohibition was enacted in the United States in 1920, the manufacture, sale and transportation of alcoholic beverages in the United States was outlawed. Bootlegging foreign-made product became an important method of getting alcoholic beverages to American consumers. Canadian distillers suddenly had a huge advantage over their American competitors as the demand for their products skyrocketed. A previously insignificant company located on the Detroit River on the east side of Windsor, *Hiram Walker*, took full advantage of its border location and proximity to a major American city. The influx of money from bootlegged "Canadian Club" whiskey allowed Hiram Walker to expand rapidly. A suburb of higher-end homes was developed stretching to the south of the plant and west of Walker Road to house company executives and other employees. The area became known as Walkerville.

With the start of the Great Depression in 1930 and the repeal of Prohibition in 1933, both Windsor and Detroit experienced several lean years. The economy recovered in the late thirties and early forties, but Windsor was dealt a major blow in 1954 when Ford moved its Canadian headquarters and the bulk of its manufacturing to Oakville, Ontario. However, as North America experienced widespread post-war prosperity in the fifties, sixties, and seventies, Windsor continued to grow, albeit at a slow rate. The construction of the interstate highway system in the United States fuelled a growing demand for automobiles, and, prior to the energy crisis of 1973, Japanese and European auto manufacturers were unable to significantly penetrate the North American market.

All was not well in Detroit, however. Racial tensions reached the boiling point in 1967, when widespread rioting broke out and much of Detroit burned to the ground. Many Detroiters fled the city for the suburbs or greener pastures farther a field. The city has never recovered. Its population of two million in the mid sixties has been reduced to one million.

Throughout the sixties, seventies, eighties, and nineties, Windsor's experience was more benign than Detroit's. Ontario's population and economic growth was solid, fuelled by immigration to Toronto and stimulative federal and provincial fiscal policies. Canada as a whole benefited from the Cold War because of its strategic location on the most direct route between the US and the USSR. To bolster Canada's support in the struggle for strategic supremacy, prices paid by the United States for commodities and manufactured goods supplied by Canada were held high. The financial benefit was redistributed throughout the country by government taxation and spending. Toronto, in particular, benefited as the home of the big banks, which provided financing for the profitable commodity enterprises. The standard of living of the average Canadian equaled or exceeded that of the average American during this period.

Nevertheless, as a city almost totally dependent on manufacturing, Windsor was vulnerable to negative developments. In the nineties a casino was built in downtown Windsor in an attempt to diversify the economy, with limited success.

A number of seemingly unrelated geopolitical events have conspired since the mid-eighties to hammer Canadian standards of living. These events have hit Windsor particularly hard.

The fall of the Soviet Union was not the first of these events, but it was arguably the most important and fundamental. Suddenly, Canada was no longer of strategic military importance to the United States. Furthermore, socialism lost its primary sponsor state, a blow to the "mixed economy" concept, which had been employed in Canada to redistribute the wealth generated by commodity exports. Commodity prices began to fall, and the business class was emboldened to call for tax and spending cuts along with other market-based policies.

Free trade between Canada and the United States slightly preceded the fall of the USSR, but was actually prompted by it. It was motivated by a combination of greed and fear on the part of the Canadian business class, who recognized that the imminent fall of the USSR posed a huge threat and an opportunity. The fear was that, in response to the deterioration of Canada's strategic importance, the US would close the border to imports of Canadian manufactured products. This would hurt the value of all Canadian businesses, allowing US interests to take over Canadian companies for cents on the dollar. The opportunity that was identified was an attempt to take advantage of the victory of capitalism over socialism and to argue for free trade between Canada and the US, something that Canadians, including the business class, had rejected ever since Confederation. If Canadian and American companies could be given equal status within a North American market,

Canadian companies would be able to compete with American companies and maintain their market values.

The third key event was the American response to the rise of Islamic fundamentalism, culminating in the World Trade Center disaster on September 11, 2001. The roots of this movement pre-date the fall of the USSR, but its growth was stimulated as the US achieved sole superpower status. The movement was spawned by British and American middle-east policy. During the Cold War, American support of Israel against the Palestinians was maintained ostensibly for strategic reasons: Israel was a bulwark against the USSR and against the Arab states that were, or could be, aligned with the USSR. Like Canada, Israel's economy benefited greatly during this period, and Israel received billions of dollars in foreign aid from the US annually. However, America continued to side with Israel even after the Cold War ended and billions of dollars continued to flow from the United States to Israel. The US also propped up pro-American governments in several key Arab countries against the wishes of the majority of their populations. The American interest in doing so was transparent: oil and its strategic significance.

As the sole superpower following the collapse of the Soviet Union, the United States was able to wield military and economic power as never before. There was no longer a Soviet counterbalance to American influence in the middle-east. Islamic militants took on the challenge of limiting American power in the middle-east by striking back wherever and whenever possible.

The American response to 9/11 and Islamic terrorism in general as orchestrated by George W. Bush and his advisors was opportunistic, if not effective. After invading and subduing Afghanistan, the US administration asserted its right to wage pre-emptive war against any country that it identified as a threat. First on the list: Iraq. As is clearly demonstrated in Michael Moore's documentary *Fahrenheit 9/11*, the war was a kind of gangland hit executed by one family (the Bushes) on behalf of their allies (the Saudi royal family) against a rival family (Saddam Hussein). Saddam Hussein had been an ally until 1990 when he invaded Kuwait, posing a direct threat to the Saudis.

Of course, it would have been difficult for George W. Bush to garner domestic (let alone international) support for an invasion of Iraq on these grounds, or for the other motivating reasons, which included controlling the Iraqi oilfields, weakening the challenge to Israel in the middle east, funneling American taxpayer money to oil and gas interests and military contractors, and building upon the domestic political support for a "war president." So Bush and his advisors concocted a story of weapons of mass destruction and promoted it using the most sophisticated and effective propaganda machinery in history.

But how can these world events, important as they are, have any bearing on conditions in the city of Windsor, or on the Windsor rental market? The answer is that Windsor has been affected by these events much more than any other Canadian city, and probably more than any city in North America, other than New York.

The most important impact on Windsor stemming from the war on terror has been the progressive closing of the US border since 9/11. Like a gun-type nozzle on a garden hose, the US government has gradually been releasing its grip on the trigger that facilitates the flow of people through the Windsor tunnel and Ambassador bridge. The restriction on this flow has come in the form of tightened documentation requirements, and more thorough, and therefore slower, border checks. This has had a widespread and negative effect on the city's economy and quality of life. Manufacturing companies in Windsor have been directly affected by difficulties in supplying their customers in the US. Visitors from Detroit and other Midwest cities have been discouraged from crossing the border, resulting in losses for the city's bars, restaurants and stores. Trucks looking for shortcuts to avoid backups at the border periodically clog Windsor's downtown streets, filling the downtown area with exhaust and noise and tearing up the city's streets.

On the manufacturing side, Windsor has lost its competitive advantage over other Ontario cities since it is no longer significantly quicker to ship goods across the border from Windsor, because of the border delays. In fact, manufacturers located east of London have an advantage since they can easily cross the border at Sarnia by way of highway 402.

Rising energy costs, another consequence of American mid-east policy, have also hammered the Windsor economy. Is it possible that a US administration, dominated as it is by oilmen from Texas, may have foreseen the effect of the Iraq invasion on energy prices and oil and gas industry profits? Be that as it may, there is no doubt that a massive transfer of wealth is occurring from ordinary citizens to the energy sector in both Canada and the US This is also manifested as a flow of wealth from Ontario to Alberta. The cost of energy is not the only negative effect on the people and businesses of Ontario cities such as Windsor. The indirect effects are probably even more damaging. As a petrodollar, the loonie has risen dramatically, damaging the competitiveness of Canadian manufacturers and discouraging tourism. Ostensibly to dampen the overheated Alberta economy, the Bank of Canada has jacked up interest rates, putting further upward pressure on the dollar. The high cost of gasoline has discouraged consumers from purchasing big trucks, minivans and SUVs, vehicles that are the bread and butter of the US automakers. The negative effects of all of these factors are focused directly, like a perfect storm, on Windsor.

Interestingly, the energy boom that is centred in Alberta and the other western provinces has not hurt Toronto. In fact, Toronto has benefited because Canadian banking regulations require the western energy companies to finance their expansion through the Toronto banks. Of course, if Canadian banks were to face competition from New York or Chicago for this business it's easy to imagine that this could throw Toronto into depression.

On the economic diversification front, Windsor is having more and more difficulty attracting American visitors because of the border tightening and the increase in the value of the loonie. The city received a brief shot in the arm when *SuperBowl XL* was held in Detroit in early February 2006. However, there was an outcry from city officials when an article about Windsor published in a Detroit newspaper prior to the superbowl dubbed Windsor "sin city." No, the officials insisted, Windsor is about families and a safe, wholesome lifestyle, not strip clubs, body rub parlours and "after hours" clubs. This blatant hypocrisy was ignored by superbowl celebrants, who came to Windsor in droves looking for a good time.

In response to Windsor's problems, the Ontario government through the Ontario Gaming and Lottery Commission (OGLC) announced in 2005 that a $400 million expansion of Windsor Casino would be built by 2008. The expansion includes a 400-room hotel, a 100,000-square-foot convention center, and a 5,000-seat auditorium. Ostensibly, the expansion is intended to attract visitors who intend to stay in the city for several days, but it will be difficult to achieve that goal. The reason is that the Bush administration is set to hammer the final nail into cross border traffic's coffin by introducing a passport requirement for anyone entering the US. This measure was initially intended to apply to vehicle passengers in January 2008, but appears to have been delayed to 2009. It means that any American visiting Canada will need to have a passport or other approved secure document to get back home. A notoriously low percentage of Americans hold passports, and it's doubtful that Americans will go to the trouble of getting a passport just so they can visit Windsor. Any American company or organization that proposes holding a convention in Windsor will face an internal revolt because of the passport requirement. Therefore, the $400 million investment appears to be intended strictly as a construction project, designed to give Windsor's economy a short-term shot in the arm.

The grim effects of the geopolitical forces and the mismanagement of the city are most clearly measured by the stagnation of property values in the city, particularly in the downtown area. While property values in most cities in Ontario, and indeed throughout Canada and the rest of the world, have escalated at nearly double-digit annual rates over the past ten years, Windsor has experienced stagnant or falling real estate prices. Essentially, this amounts to a 50% decline in property values in downtown Windsor relative to everywhere else in just a decade. In a market-based economy such as Ontario's, this represents a staggering vote of non-confidence not only in the city's current situation, but even more in its prospects for the future. In this vein, it's worth pointing out that a real estate survey published in June, 2006, showed that Windsor was the only major market in which luxury home sales were down in the first half of the year. The number of such sales in the first half of 2006 was a piddling 4, compared with 250 in the Greater Toronto Area. Now it's true that the population of the GTA is much greater than Windsor, by a factor of 20 or so, but even so the number of luxury home sales in Windsor, per capita, is relatively tiny. However, these figures actually inflate the Windsor statistics drastically. The reason is that a luxury home in Toronto is defined as one whose selling price exceeds $1.5 million, whereas the luxury price threshold in Windsor is defined as $0.5 million. In other words, it's almost impossible to sell a home in Windsor for one-third of the price of a similar home that would likely spark a bidding war in Toronto.

To summarize the situation, the auto industry, which for decades has been the foundation of the Windsor economy, is in a tailspin. A strategy was developed to diversify into gambling and entertainment, but has foundered in the wake of 9/11. What can be done?

First, the possibility that nothing can be done, and that Windsor will continue to decay, has to be acknowledged. We have observed an attitude of resignation, and even a desire for continuing deterioration among the populace, middle class and low-income alike. There is a strong blue-collar ethos in Windsor that has somehow fed just as strong a welfare ethos. However, as a starting point for a hypothetical renaissance, it's worthwhile to consider any advantages the city may have. These include:

- Closing of the US border may initiate an increasingly Canada-first mentality. There may be increased economic and social contact between Windsor and Toronto that could at least partly offset the loss of Windsor's status as a suburb of Detroit.

- Windsor has the warmest winter weather in Canada outside of British Columbia. It is noticeably milder than Toronto. We've seen roses in bloom in early December, and enjoyed shirtsleeve weather in March and April when Toronto was 10°C cooler. It's not a great place for winter sports. Unfortunately, Windsor's winter climate could not be described as mild.

- Real estate prices are extremely low and land is almost free, which would normally present opportunities for investors.

- Windsor has a university.

The first priority is to develop office jobs in downtown Windsor. The industrial sector is shrinking, and the entertainment industry has been dealt a killing blow by the aftereffects of 9/11. Clearly, if there is any town that could get a boost from office development it is Windsor. There is some reason to hope that this can happen. For example, the University of Windsor is close to the downtown, and could act as a catalyst for the growth of companies in the health care or auto design businesses. The Ontario government has decided to open a medical school at the university, which will initially be small, but is expected to create spin-off business activity. However, to realize a significant fraction of the potential benefits, the university will have to lose its reputation as the school of last resort for students who cannot qualify for any other university in Ontario. It's well known that the University of Windsor has one of the lowest average entrance grade requirements in Ontario, and perennially ranks at or near the bottom of *Maclean's* annual survey of Canadian universities.

The reality is that the world has passed Windsor by. Windsor has become a full-fledged member of the Midwest rust belt, even as the border with the United States is closing. The blue-collar ethos is deep-seated, even as blue-collar workers stream out of the city, headed for Alberta. What lies ahead in ten or twenty years if the slide is not reversed?

One impact of the slide in property values in downtown Windsor is that even basic repairs become uneconomic, so that the condition of many houses and buildings will deteriorate rapidly. For example, a typical duplex in the Toronto area valued at $500,000 has been appreciating at a double-digit rate for the past several years. A $20,000 repair or renovation is not a big deal as it can be financed out of less than one year's appreciation. On the other hand, virtually the same duplex, on a much bigger lot, in downtown Windsor, would have sold for $140,000 prior to 9/11, and, assuming it is in good condition, would be lucky to fetch $100,000 in 2007. It's impossible to justify pouring $20,000 into repairs for such a property. On the other hand, if the owner were to try to sell the property, a prospective buyer would subtract the cost of the repairs, as well as a further penalty of $10,000 to $20,000 for insurance against the falling property values and the difficulty in finding suitable tenants, for an offer price of $60,000 to $70,000. If the city tries to force repairs to be made, the owner has to pay out of his own pocket or walk away from the property, forcing a foreclosure.

Arguably, at some point a buyer may acquire the property for a low enough price that repairs can be economic, but it's not clear at what point this will happen, or if it will happen. There is a feedback between the deteriorating housing stock and the disappearance of the middle class population in downtown Windsor. There is no end in sight to this trend. As blue-collar workers pour out of Windsor, they are replaced by a flock of low-income people dependent on the city for support. Downtown Windsor has become a low-income haven, having more in common with the big subsidized housing developments in Toronto such as Regent Park than with a small city.

Supporting the influx of low-income people dependent on social services puts a huge strain on the city's budget. Police and fire services are cut back, just when they are needed the most. As a result, downtown Windsor will increasingly become a no man's land with the city having minimal capability to encourage or enforce order. Interestingly, the Ontario property tax assessment system is doing its part to minimize the burden on Windsor's suburban residents of supporting the downtown's burgeoning welfare population. This is being accomplished by systematically over-valuing properties in the downtown area. The most recent assessment, done in January 2005, found that the average Windsor residential property increased by 3% since the previous assessment done in 2003. However, the assessments on our downtown properties increased by an average of 7.4% over the same period. This occurred at a time when property values in downtown Windsor were clearly dropping. Furthermore, we've checked the assessments on similar properties in the downtown area and found that they are systematically over-valued. In some cases, we estimate that the assessments are 50% higher than the price that a property could get on the real estate market. The property tax assessments are supposed to be "actual value" assessments, so discrepancies of the magnitude we've seen are inexcusable.

Ironically, Ontario waterfront property owners are the group most vocally upset with the property tax assessment system. Their assessments have risen dramatically. However, their property values have also skyrocketed—faster, we suspect, than their assessments have increased. So, although these property owners are very likely underpaying taxes, they are in the forefront of a movement to scrap the actual value system. Meanwhile, property owners in downtown Windsor, who are being grossly overtaxed, get no credibility or attention because their assessments have risen modestly. To add insult to injury, the Ontario government has responded to the complaints of the waterfront property owners as well as others by freezing all assessments for an additional year.

Returning to the low-income demographic of downtown Windsor, we have heard rumours that Windsor social services has recently been providing welfare recipients with financial packages to relocate to Toronto or Calgary. While we haven't been able to confirm this rumour, it's easy to imagine that city council is alarmed by the deep erosion of the property tax base and by the need to fund an ever-growing phalanx of social service recipients. Perhaps they have had enough. And if it is true that welfare recipients are being shipped out of Windsor, it must be going on with the approval of the provincial government, and perhaps even the federal government. This, in turn, is a clear indication of the urgency of the crisis facing Windsor.

9

Case VI—My Brother Darrell And My Other Brother Darrell

We had just evicted a couple from one of our rental units. During their stay, their pit bull had gone through both windows at the front of our house, chasing cats, dogs or people, so we were really hoping that we would be able to find better tenants. There have got to be some good tenants out there—right? ... Wrong! We showed the unit to a couple of young guys in their early twenties who showed up at one of our showings. They seemed reasonably acceptable. One of them had a smell of alcohol on his breath, but he wasn't drunk. The showing was at 6:30 p.m. on a Saturday, so he might have just had a beer with his dinner. They filled out the application and gave us a deposit as well. When we got home we did a credit check and found that all of their particulars panned out. They both had good jobs, which we confirmed by talking to their employers. Nothing seemed amiss, so we decided to accept them. They didn't have any pit bulls, just two cats. We thought, "Great, maybe we won't have to deal with any more broken windows."

Soon after they moved in, we visited the place on a weekend. We noticed some carpet lying out in the backyard. It was about 4 feet wide and 6 feet long. Looking at it a little closer, we realized it was the carpeting from the small hallway between the two bedrooms of the main unit. It had a distinct pattern. We knocked on the front door and the tenant who had smelled of alcohol on his breath came to the door. We'll call him "my brother Darrell." When we asked him why the carpet was in the backyard, he said, "Because the cats sprayed on it." Any other landlord would have hit the ceiling but we tended to have a lot of patience, a trait that has since diminished. We politely asked him to check with us first if they intended to do anything like that in the future. We would have to okay it.

The next time we visited, we noticed rolled-up carpet inside the enclosed fire escape at the back of the house. We again checked it out. This time it was the living room carpeting from the same unit. We knocked on the front door again, and "my brother Darrell" answered the door again. We asked him about the carpeting and he said they preferred the hardwood floors. We asked to take a look. We had to admit the hardwood floors looked pretty nice. We asked him if there was anything else they were thinking of changing. He said "No." We told him we would have to take legal action against them next time if they didn't check with us first. We ended up storing the carpet in the basement for future use.

"My brother Darrell" said he would mow the lawn for us and seemed to be trying to give a good impression. They both reminded us of two young boys who might have had behavioural problems and wanted to prove they could be decent young men. We were willing to give them a chance, even though they would have to be told "NO!" once in awhile.

One weekend, we showed the vacant upper unit to someone who had been a tenant of ours in the past, a woman named Karen. She had been a good tenant. The only drawback was that she was the sister of Carol who wreaked so much havoc in case IV—"the Eve of Destruction." Karen always kept her unit clean and never did any significant damage. She did have a tendency to exaggerate the transgressions of other tenants in neighbouring units.

While we were showing Karen the upper unit, music was blaring from the main floor unit where "my brother Darrell" and his room-mate "my other brother Darrell" lived. We thought "Oh no, not again." Even though Karen could hear the loud music, she rented the upper unit anyway. We told her that we would tell the tenant below to keep the music down. After she left, we told the girlfriend of "my brother Darrell" that they were not allowed to play their music that loud. On future visits, when they had no idea we were coming, we found that the music was always quieter.

Karen moved in but started to complain about the Darrells. Because of her past record of exaggerating, it was hard to know if her complaints were legitimate. Her biggest complaint was the loud music. When we would ask the brothers about it, they would reply that she was exaggerating.

The brothers started to be late paying their rent and "my brother Darrell" told us that he had been laid off and was applying for unemployment insurance. The brothers did eventually pay their rent but continued to pay late in the following months.

Karen called and told us that a window had been broken in "my brother Darrell's" car, which was unlicensed and immobile in the rear parking area. She said there was broken glass lying all over the parking area and they hadn't cleaned it up yet. We called "my brother Darrell" and asked him to please clean up the glass. He said it had just happened and he would clean it up immediately. Karen called again in a few days. They still hadn't cleaned up the glass. When we visited the property a few days later, the glass was still there. There were also stacks of wood and old bikes in the backyard. We finally got "my brother Darrell" to clean up the glass, although the wood and bikes never disappeared.

One evening Karen called and said that the Darrells had destroyed the front porch. We said "What?" She said that they had been hammering or knocking on the bricks of the front porch every once in awhile. She didn't know for sure what they were up to until she saw loose mortar sitting in piles on the porch. It dawned on her that they were loosening the bricks. It struck us as odd that she had never mentioned this to us before. That night, before Karen called us, they had been having a party, sitting on the porch, kicking at the bricks until the wall caved in. We called the police. The police were of no help and told us that they believed that the porch was falling apart, something that was true only due to the actions of the Darrells.

According to the brothers, when we reached them by phone, they had no idea what Karen was talking about with regard to their "picking away at the mortar." It was a complete surprise to them that the porch caved in. "My other brother Darrell" was a bricklayer, and he offered to repair the porch. We told him it would have to be done to our satisfaction … at no cost to us.

We called our paralegal and asked her to drop by and take some pictures for us. After we looked at the pictures we couldn't believe the damage.

By now, we were thinking that we had to get rid of these jokers. Maybe it was our stupidity, but we tended to give them the benefit of the doubt because they were likable. At least they usually repaired the things they damaged. That was much more than Karen's sister Carol ever did. "My brother Darrell" even put some laminated flooring down in the hallway where they had taken out the 4-by-6 foot carpet. However, the cumulative effect of the damage and troublemaking finally came to a head, and we finally had to serve the brothers an N5 notice for disturbing the peace. Our neighbours complained that they would sit on the front porch drinking and would yell out to people walking by. We were surprised that they hadn't been beaten up, or killed. They eventually didn't pay their rent and we had to evict them. We suspected that they had been going into the basement, which was not part of their unit. It always looked as though someone had been rummaging around down there, where we store a lot of our things. They had made a hole through a wall that, at one time, had a door leading down to the basement.

After we regained possession of the unit, we found that the brothers Darrell had modified the wiring in the house. The living room had no ceiling light fixture, so they took it upon themselves to install one, in the laziest way possible. They took electrical cable with a jury-rigged electrical switch and plug, and plugged it into a wall outlet. They ran the cable across the ceiling and connected it to a light fixture that was screwed to a piece of plywood that, in turn, was screwed to the ceiling. The light fixture and the switch were installed without benefit of an electrical box. Needless to say, that is a gross violation of the building code that could have resulted in electrocution of the brothers Darrell (no such luck) or one of their guests, or might have caused a fire that could have burned the house down. They had also tapped electrical cables into ceiling lights in the unfinished basement and run the cables into their main floor unit. It wasn't clear what they were using the cables for, but a marijuana grow-op comes to mind as a possibility. It cost us $300 to get an electrician to undo the changes they had made to the wiring.

Bikes, wood and other debris dumped by the Darrells at the back of the house.

Bricks kicked out of the front porch by the Darrells.

Damage to the front porch caused by the Darrells.

10

Case VII—The Three Faces of Eve: Adam and Eve

We first found out about Eve when one of our tenants named Patsy told us she knew of someone who might be interested in renting the upper unit that was vacant above hers. We asked Patsy who this person was and Patsy said that she didn't know her directly, but she was a friend of a friend. We'll call her Eve.

We set up an appointment with Eve for her to view the unit. We arrived at the unit on the day and at the time of the appointment, but she didn't show up. We should have seen a red flag because of this, but we checked with Patsy and she said she would call Eve. Apparently she was at the hospital with her daughter (we realized later that the hospital was an excuse she made use of quite a bit). She said she would be there in half an hour. We waited. She finally showed up, viewed the unit and said she loved it. The only problem was that we had already showed it to another person and she had taken an application form. We didn't know if she would come back with the application and a deposit, but in the end she did.

We called Eve and told her that we had another unit for her, but it wasn't ready yet as it needed painting. The tenant who had recently left the unit had said that he would paint, but never did. Eve looked at it within a few days and wanted to move in right away. We told her we could agree to that but she would have to let us in to do the painting and repairs. She agreed. Eve was on Ontario Works and said she would not have a problem with the rent, as Ontario Works would pay for anywhere she wanted to live. Her daughter had several significant medical problems, so Eve had to be at home to take care of her daughter. She said she couldn't pay last month's rent as she had to buy a diabetic pump for her daughter, but she agreed to make payments. She seemed really nice and very believable so we decided to rent to her, even though her caseworker warned us to get "pay direct." With pay direct, her Ontario Works check would be mailed directly to us. When a caseworker tells a landlord this, the landlord's antenna goes up, but for some reason Eve seemed so nice that we were willing to go ahead with her.

Within the next month we had made several appointments with Eve to come in and paint and do some minor repairs, but Eve ended up canceling on us each time. One excuse was that she had been up all night with her daughter at the hospital and she didn't have the energy for us to come in.

Another excuse that Eve used was that she had a gravelly voice and she said she had laryngitis. After the third excuse, we decided to ask her if she wanted to paint, and she agreed to do so. It was at about this time that she started getting bitchier. Soon afterward, we got an order in the mail from the Windsor building department to do some repairs on her unit. One of the items identified in the order was to have the Electrical Safety Authority inspect the unit, as the building inspector found multiple extension cords plugged into a single receptacle, and wall plates were missing from some of the electrical outlets. We had taken a few wall plates off the wall to paint just before Eve moved in and, because we were trying to get the unit painted and Eve had agreed to paint, we hadn't put them back on yet. It costs the landlord $200 to have the Electrical Safety Authority inspect a property.

The property had been inspected two years earlier by the Electrical Safety Authority after we had a fire in the house (see Chapter 4), so luckily the certificate we got from that inspection was still valid. When we pointed this out to the building inspector, he agreed that we didn't have to contact the ESA as long as our electrician made any necessary repairs. Eileen checked with Eve to see if she had called the building department but she denied it. She said they just showed up at her door wanting to inspect the house. We asked the inspector who had called for the inspection, but he said he couldn't divulge that information.

When we visited the house the next day, a large, intimidating boyfriend that we had never met before was visiting Eve. We'll call him Adam. We also noticed a large attack dog, whereas Eve had a small dog. When we questioned Eve about the strange dog, she said that she had to get rid of the small dog because it wasn't able to protect her.

Adam pointed out that the electrical cover plates weren't on the wall. Eileen quickly pointed out that Eve had agreed to paint and that we hadn't put them back. Eve coyly asked Adam if he would paint for her. He agreed. Adam was also quick to point out that there were loose boards on the front porch and a few other problems. We quickly realized that Eve had undoubtedly called the building department at the urging of her new boyfriend, a conclusion that was not really in doubt before that.

We had brought our electrician with us and he said he could put in a new plug so that Adam and Eve wouldn't have as many extension cords. We agreed to let him do this.

Soon after this visit Eve's toilet overflowed and we had to call a plumber out to the house to unplug it. He had to come back a second time as it overflowed again and he said there were a lot of tampons plugging it. Eve denied using tampons, and a few minutes later we also got a call from Adam. When Eileen answered the phone he very rudely said, "Who's this?" When Eileen replied, "Who's this?" (even though she recognized his voice) he identified himself. He asked, "When is this toilet going to get fixed?" When Eileen explained that she talks to the tenant, not the boyfriend, Adam wouldn't calm down. She had to hang up on him and then he called back five minutes later. Eileen tried to be very nice to him, and said that she had called the plumbing company again and that they said they would put a camera down the sewer pipe to see what the problem was.

Eve called again and told Charles that when the toilet had backed up, the Christmas presents she had bought were damaged. This was in October! As Eve talked, Charles could hear Adam prompting her in the background, saying things like "We don't have to take shit like this." A few days later, after Eve had calmed down, Charles offered to check out the damage to the Christmas presents, and possibly help pay for new ones. "No problem, I threw the old ones out and bought new ones," was Eve's reply.

The sewer problem was solved but Eve continued to be her bitchy alter ego. One weekend, Charles went to the unit to do some repairs. Eve let Charles in the front door, and he went back to the kitchen to work. A few minutes later, he finished the work and wanted to discuss the work that he had done with Eve, but could only find her daughter in the living room. Charles asked the daughter where Eve was, and without answering, the daughter led Charles to the nearby bedroom door. The daughter opened the door and Charles, who had followed right behind the daughter, couldn't help seeing Adam and Eve in bed together. They didn't seem to be the least bit concerned to see Charles standing there with a surprised look on his face. They acted as though this was the norm for them, to be in bed in the middle of the afternoon while a repair was being done.

Charles replaced a few boards on the porch, but within one week our repairman called to say that one of the boards had been broken. The boards were two by six pressure treated wood, similar to the original ones. Charles was checking out the damage on the porch when the tenant from the other unit appeared. She told Charles that Adam, a man of generous proportions, had been jumping up and down on one foot, causing the board to break.

Later that month Eileen got a call from a landlord asking for a reference for Eve as she had applied to rent from him. He didn't leave a number to call back. Eileen phoned Eve to ask her about the call, as Eve hadn't informed Eileen or Charles that she was moving. Eve responded, "At the end of the month—I'm out of here." When Eileen said she had to give sixty days notice Eve just said, "I'll be out by the end of the month."

Eileen called Ontario Works to let them know Eve hadn't given sixty days notice. They just said "Talk to the Province—we don't deal with that, we just send the check."

Experienced landlords will recognize this story because it happens over and over. A new tenant seems to be one of the nicest people you've ever met. Suddenly, she has a new boyfriend and Dr. Jekyll becomes Ms. Hyde. The building inspector is called (boyfriend says she shouldn't have to live in a dump like this, and maybe she can get a rent abatement for maintenance problems), there's a new dog (boyfriend says it's a bad neighbourhood and she needs protection—his attack dog) and the sewer suddenly backs up (boyfriend says we should put some tampons down the toilet, overflow it, and try to get compensation for some nonexistent Christmas presents).

Regarding toilets backing up, many tenants tend to be rather blasé about what gets into the toilet. One tenant called two days after we took possession of a house, complaining that her toilet was blocked. The plumber found a towel in the toilet. We were naïve at the time and fixed it without confronting her, but nowadays there is a nasty argument when a tenant tries to pull a stunt like that. Other items we have found in backed up toilets, besides the ever-popular tampon, include deodorant sticks, kids' toys and condoms.

11

Case VIII—Of Rats and Men: Stephanie

Our first contact with Stephanie occurred when she replied to our ad in the *Windsor Star* about our little detached house. She said she was living in a house behind a strip club and she had to move because of the noise and other unpleasant activities. She asked if we would allow her to have two dogs. We sometimes say yes to one dog, depending on the breed (actually the Board's rules do not permit a landlord to refuse a tenant on the basis of pets, and don't prohibit a tenant from lying about pets to get a rental unit). Eileen asked Stephanie what kind of dog she had, and Stephanie replied that they were both boxers. One was fifteen years old. Eileen said that one dog would be acceptable, but that she was concerned that the old dog would have wetting accidents and damage the carpets in the house.

A prospective tenant called the next day and talked to Charles, telling him her name was Stephanie. Although Eileen had mentioned her call the previous day, she hadn't described all of the details to Charles, so he was not aware that this was the same Stephanie who had talked to Eileen. When Charles asked her if she had any pets, she said she had **one** dog. After Charles got off the phone, Eileen asked him who had called and he told her it was someone named Stephanie. When Eileen called her back to set up an appointment to see the house, she thought the voice was the same as the one who called the day before. Eileen asked her if she was the same Stephanie who had called the previous day and who had two dogs. Stephanie denied it.

After doing a credit check we accepted Stephanie as a tenant, on the condition that we receive her monthly rent payments by direct pay from Windsor social services. Both Stephanie and social services agreed to this.

Stephanie seemed nice, but Eileen couldn't shake the feeling that she was the same Stephanie who had said she had two dogs. On a visit that we paid to Stephanie a few days after she moved in, her little daughter said to Eileen, "Guess what? We have two dogs." When Eileen asked Stephanie about it she said that she was only pet sitting the other dog for three days.

One month later, on November 1, Stephanie called and said that she saw a rat in the kitchen and that it was after her children's Halloween candy. Eileen immediately called a pest control company and they came out to the house and put down bait and traps. There was a hole in the wall beside the kitchen cupboard where the rat had gotten into the house. The pest control people advised us not to close the hole immediately to allow the traps to work. A few days later, we plugged up the hole. We found a hole in the ground under the edge of the patio at the side of the house where a rat had likely burrowed into the crawl space under the house. The pest control people put rat poison in the crawl space, and they advised us that if a rat were killed by the poison and died in the crawl space it would probably start smelling. We decided to wait a few days before closing off the opening under the patio.

A week later we placed patio stones over sheet metal to eliminate access to the crawl space from the side patio. Stephanie didn't mention any smells at that time, but a week later she complained that she could smell decaying rats. Eileen advised her to get some air fresheners and we would reimburse her for them. Stephanie didn't complain of the smell during the last two weeks of November, and Charles didn't smell anything when he visited the house during this time.

By December 4, we had not yet received the December rent payment from social services. Eileen called Stephanie, and she said that for some reason the money had been deposited into her bank account. She didn't know why. She had the money at the house, but wouldn't be there for us to pick it up, as she had to take her daughter to girl guides.

The next morning Eileen went grocery shopping. When she arrived back home, there were two phone messages from Stephanie saying that we had to come right now and smell the odour from the rats. Eileen said that she couldn't come but would send someone over immediately. Stephanie said she wasn't sure if she had to baby sit a little girl that day and might have to go to the school to pick her up. Eileen asked Stephanie if she was babysitting or running a daycare. She said, "No, but I know what you are up to." She probably thought that we were thinking of reporting her to social services. We never said anything about reporting her and, in fact, we just wanted to know what our property was being used for. Eileen mentioned that we noticed quite a few children's playthings in the backyard. Stephanie grew agitated and said, "How dare you ask me that?" Eileen mentioned to Stephanie that she had brought up the subject herself and that we have the right to know if she's babysitting on our property. The phone went dead.

As an aside, it could be argued (by tenant's rights groups) that whether or not Stephanie was running a daycare is none of our business. To prohibit such an activity would violate her rights and freedoms, and in any case there is nothing we could do about it if she continued. However, if our property insurance company were to find out about it, they would not be happy about it and, at the very least they would increase our premiums. More likely, they would cut us off. If one of Stephanie's clients were injured on the property, it would be a catastrophe for us. As usual, we the landlord are stuck in the middle, held responsible for the actions of our tenants although we have no control over those actions.

Stephanie called back and asked why Eileen hung up on her. Eileen said she didn't hang up, and the phone just went dead. Stephanie started getting agitated again. Eileen said she would call the pest people again to see if they could put bait down that would dissolve the rats when they ate it.

Eileen called our handyman after finishing the conversation with Stephanie and asked him to stop by Stephanie's place to collect the rent and to see if he could detect any odours from the rats. He called Eileen and said that Stephanie refused to pay him—she said she wanted to pay us directly. He said he checked for odours and found none. In Eileen's mind, Stephanie's credibility was in question. Eileen also called the pest people to ask them if they had bait that would dissolve the rats. They said they didn't have such a product, but would go over to the house to check on things.

Eileen also called Stephanie's caseworker and asked her why we had not received the "pay direct" rent cheque. She said the cheque had been withheld by request of the tenant, because of a rat problem. Eileen told the caseworker that rent could not be withheld and that the tenant could file with the Tribunal and get a rent rebate if it ruled in her favour. The caseworker said the tenant was her customer, and she had to do what the customer requested. Eileen called the Tribunal and asked an employee to confirm what Eileen already knew, that the rent couldn't be withheld and that the tenant could file a complaint. When Eileen asked the Tribunal employee if she could call or fax the caseworker and tell her this, she said she couldn't. She said that the Tribunal staff don't make outside calls or faxes. Because of this silly rule, this could lead to a hearing in six weeks, cost to the landlord for application fees and for legal help, time off work for the landlord to attend the hearing, etc.

Eileen called the caseworker again, and left a message on the caseworker's answering machine to inform her that Eileen had called the Tribunal and that they (the Tribunal) had agreed with Eileen that the tenant couldn't hold back the rent. Eileen stated that the caseworker didn't know the rules and that we felt like suing her personally for doing whatever the tenant asked for. Eileen called our paralegal to issue an N4 (an eviction notice for nonpayment of rent) to Stephanie and also to fax a letter to the caseworker. The letter stated that Stephanie had lied about what happened to her welfare payment for the rent.

On the sixth of the month, our paralegal got a call from Stephanie saying she could pick up the rent. She went over to Stephanie's that afternoon and picked up the rent. She said she didn't notice any smell, but there were frogs in a container and Stephanie admitted they hadn't been cleaned in a while.

Two days later, Stephanie called at 2:00 in the afternoon and said she had Union Energy at the house. She said she had smelled something and they had found a faulty valve on the water heater. The technician said he couldn't fix it and the owner would have to call someone to fix it. Stephanie said, "See, I told you there was a smell." Eileen said, "Stephanie, you complained there was a rat smell. If you suspected gas, why didn't you mention gas, and I would have called Union Gas." Stephanie kept arguing. Eileen said she would have to hang up. Stephanie kept arguing and Eileen finally raised her voice. Stephanie said, "You're raising your voice—I have a witness that you're yelling." Eileen repeated, "Stephanie, I need you to hang up so I can call Union Gas."

Stephanie finally hung up, but before she did, she asked when a repairman would be out to fix the valve. Eileen called the Union Gas emergency number, and they said they had already told Stephanie they would be out within the hour.

Eileen tried calling Stephanie back, at least four times. The line was busy. Finally after ten minutes the line was free and Eileen told Stephanie that Union Gas would be at the house within the hour. When Eileen told Stephanie the guy from Union Gas already told her they would be out within the hour she argued and said they hadn't told her that.

Before 3:00 Eileen realized if there was a problem they (Union Gas) wouldn't be able to reach her, as she would be out of the house for an hour, so she decided to call Union Gas to leave her cell phone number. The lady said there was no work order from Union Gas. Eileen suspected it had been Union Gas that had been at the house, not Union Energy, so Eileen called Union Energy, the water heater rental company. They said they would come out the next day to fix the valve since Union Gas would have shut off the gas supply to the hot water tank only, not to the rest of the house.

When Eileen got back at 4:00, Stephanie had left a phone message saying "You knew that they turned off the gas to the whole house, right?" Eileen sent our handyman Willy over to the house to check on the situation, and he confirmed that the main gas supply was, indeed, off, but that Stephanie had an electric heater to keep the house reasonably warm. Then Stephanie told Willy that she was planning to go to a friend's house for the night.

When Charles got home at 5:30, he decided to call Stephanie to make sure her situation was okay. Stephanie told him that she had called Union Energy, told them that she was without heat, and got them to come out and fix the leaking valve. She made a point of highlighting how she had insisted they come to fix the problem and got action, something Eileen failed to do. Charles pointed out that Eileen had made several calls to Union Gas and Union Energy, and that Stephanie had mistakenly told Eileen Union Energy had come out when in reality it was Union Gas, which led to a delay in dealing with the problem. Then, after we learned that the gas was shut off, we were told she was satisfied with waiting until the next day for the repair.

The next morning we called Union Energy and asked them to fax us a copy of the work order for the repair. A handwritten note on the work order stated only that a leak had been repaired with no charge to the homeowner. Since Union Energy charges for work done to parts that are not included in the rental equipment, this means that the leak occurred in the equipment rented from Union Energy.

Throughout December, every time we visited the house Charles would ask Stephanie if she had seen any more rats. She said she hadn't, and Charles didn't notice any odour even though Stephanie said she could smell an odour.

We decided to have the pest people come out monthly to put down bait as a preventative measure. Around the beginning of January when the pest people paid their monthly visit, they asked Stephanie if she had seen any more rats. She said no, but she could still smell them. The pest people reported no smell.

Stephanie called us on February 1 and said she wanted to leave at the end of the month because of the rat problem. Even though we felt that the rat problem was under control, we decided to release her from the sixty days notice requirement. We told her that we would waive the sixty days notice and she could leave at the end of the month if she wished. We told our paralegal that Stephanie would be leaving at the end of February, and she told us that she thought Stephanie would ask the Tribunal for a rent abatement. Sure enough, in early March Eileen got a call from Stephanie's legal aid assistant. She had an attitude problem (our paralegal has said that many of the legal aid assistants are in training, and they're given these kinds of cases for training, so they are trying to prove themselves).

She mentioned that Stephanie wanted to **negotiate** a rent abatement from us as she **had** to move and needed money to help her move because she was in a financial bind. She said that we were landlords and **landlords have money**. Eileen couldn't believe what she was hearing from this legal assistant. Eileen told the legal aid assistant that many people have financial problems, she didn't know what our financial situation was, and we were not willing to negotiate.

Eileen explained to the legal aid assistant that we let Stephanie leave without giving us sixty days notice, so when Stephanie called us on February 1 she had probably already received her February rent payment from social services. Stephanie did not have to pay to us for February, as she was using the last month's rent she had paid us for February, so she was probably pocketing the rent payment from social services without social services' knowledge. She was already ahead of the game but wanted more. Eileen notified our paralegal of her discussion with legal aid, and the paralegal sent a letter to the legal aid assistant about the condition of our house when Stephanie left. There were broken blinds and a broken toilet. She left behind eight hundred pounds of her junk, which we had to pay our handyman to take to the dump.

Our paralegal explained in her letter to the legal aid assistant that the damage that was done to the toilet was obviously intentional and that we would incur a cost to replace it. We do not know if Stephanie will still try to get a rent abatement as she has a year to apply to the Board. If we find out before this book is published, we'll let you know.

We phoned Stephanie's previous landlord, whom we didn't call before Stephanie became our tenant (the reason we didn't call at that time is that when a bad tenant is leaving her previous residence, the landlord usually gives her a good reference just to get rid of her). We found out that Stephanie hadn't even let the landlord know that she had left when she moved to our house. Her house had been vacant for two weeks and the landlord didn't even know it, which is certainly a liability to the landlord. Stephanie's boyfriend had kicked in the front door of her house and Stephanie had left garbage all over the place. We asked her if she would back us up in court if Stephanie decided to take us to court. We don't know if we could use her testimony as perhaps Stephanie's rights under the Privacy Act might be violated if we tried to use her previous landlord as a witness.

Stephanie's attitude throughout this episode typifies the attitude of many low-income tenants—me first. Perhaps it can be justified or at least understood because of the difficulties they have endured over the years. Perhaps they were even cheated by an unscrupulous landlord at one time or another. This might explain Stephanie's tendency to find fault with her rental home and her landlord, and her refusal to acknowledge any efforts on the part of her landlord. However, it appears to us that the social welfare and landlord-tenant systems are all too eager to encourage this attitude, by sending low-income tenants the unequivocal message "we are on your side, no matter what." Landlords on the other hand have no equivalent government support, are routinely pilloried as a group in the media, and are relegated to the courts and collection agencies in a futile attempt to gain reparation for the actions of tenants.

We often get repeated calls from prospective tenants, as was the case with Stephanie. Some have forgotten that they called the same number the previous day, and realize what they've done. Others have forgotten that they called the previous day, and probably would never realize it unless we point it out to them. Some deliberately call repeatedly for one reason or other—whether it's a scam or just a symptom of an obsessive-compulsive disorder, or some other agenda, isn't always clear.

A surprising number of callers are quite frank about their desire to get out of their current situation. Some will even voluntarily tell us that they have taken their landlord to the Board over this or that problem. It didn't take long for us to realize that we shouldn't rent to such people under any circumstances. We don't even understand why someone would brag about a dispute with their landlord, since it's doubtful that any landlord would rent to them. Can we legally turn down a prospective tenant because she is suing her current landlord? We don't know for certain, but we doubt it. On the other hand, we would have to be out of our minds to rent to such a person, and if we did so and got sued as a result any impartial observer would say we were idiots and deserved our fate.

Plastic mini blind destroyed byStephanie. This had to be done deliberately by an adult because it was at the top of the window.

Mountain of junk left behind by Stephanie.

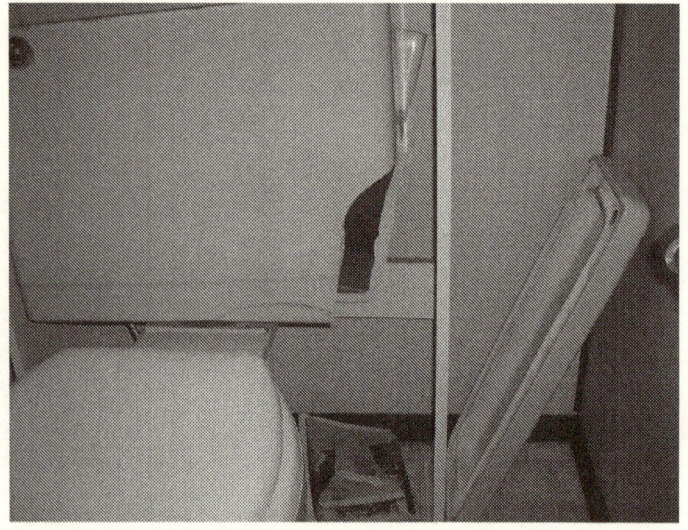

Toilet destroyed by Stephanie. This was obviously done deliberately.

12

Case IX—Sarah, Mary-Lou and Granny

We first met Sarah, and Sarah's mother Mary Lou, when we were going through a house for the first time with our realtor. The outside of the house was very drab. The wooden siding was painted gray, but the house was drastically in need of a new paint job. Even our property insurance agent asked us why we would want to buy it. The paint was peeling so badly that you could just lift it off with your finger. We wondered, "Should we go in and look at the inside or not." We decided to build up our courage and do so. We were pleasantly surprised. Mary Lou, who was just moving into the main floor unit, was putting together a brass bed. Her daughter Sarah was already living in the upper unit. Compared to the main floor unit, the upper unit was much more pleasing to the eye. It was more modern. There was even a nice glass-paned door at the top of the stairs. Sarah's grandmother was living in the basement. She was quite a character and was quick to show us her "throne." Her "throne" was a toilet, but you had to go up two steps to get to it.

We ended up buying the house, even though we had to delay the closing. The problem was related to the fact that we wanted to buy houses that were retrofitted, meeting all the fire, safety and building requirements. When we made the offer to buy the house, we stipulated that we wanted the house to be retrofitted, and the owners accepted the offer and said they would meet all the retrofit requirements. As a result, the owner had to replace the balcony and put in drywall in the basement ceiling. When the day of closing came around these tasks were not done. We said we would not close until they were finished and also asked for $2,000 in compensation for the delay. They came through with the requests and we closed a month later.

We enjoyed our new tenants for a while. We learned that all of them were related to the previous owner. After the first month, Sarah moved out (in the middle of the night), according to Granny. We didn't think about it too much at the time but we wonder if her relatives who sold us the house had her in there just to look like it was being rented, so it would attract buyers. She was probably living there rent-free, but didn't want to pay us the market rent.

When Granny moved out of the basement not too long after that, Sarah contacted us and told us how sorry she was that she had skipped out on us. She said she would appreciate it if we would let her rent the basement. She said it was much more affordable for her than the upper unit. We told her we would take her back only if she paid us the rent she owed us for the upper unit. She agreed. She turned out to be one of the biggest "pains in the ass" we had as a tenant.

Sarah had two small children in diapers and didn't bag her garbage properly. We asked all of our tenants to put their garbage in sealed containers, because of the rat problem in Windsor. Because Sarah never used containers, diapers were always strewn all over the backyard by rats, and she wouldn't re-bag any of the mess. We developed a rat problem at the house and had a tough time getting rid of them. Sarah would also leave her junky furniture outside and the city wouldn't come to pick it up. When we asked her to get rid of a couch that she had dumped in the backyard, she slyly put it in the neighbor's back-yard temporarily so we would think it was gone. Our repairman Willy let us know that she would put it back in our yard after we left the property.

She started having a houseguest; a much older man named Mickey whom she claimed was her stepfather. We think he was actually her boyfriend. He was very unpleasant and very verbally abusive. One afternoon, we were at the house doing some repairs. When we finished, we knocked on Sarah's basement door to ask her a question. Sarah opened the door and we stepped inside. We saw Mickey sitting in the living room and Eileen decided to ask Sarah who he was, and whether he was living with her. Mickey immediately jumped up and came barreling at us in a rage, as if he were going to assault us. For some reason, he didn't follow through, but Sarah immediately started a fuss, claiming that Eileen had knocked over her toddler as she came through the door. In reality, the toddler was standing in front of the door and Sarah didn't bother getting him out of the way, so as the door opened, the toddler was knocked over. "I'm going to call the police and have you charged with assault," bellowed Sarah. "That was an accident, and you should have moved him out of the way," countered Eileen.

Sarah called the police, and the police called us. After questioning us, they dropped the case. We were both amazed how two people who couldn't earn an honest dollar to save their lives could effortlessly choreograph a shakedown scam at a moment's notice. Could they have planned it in advance? If not, how were they able to improvise so quickly? Had they used the scam several times before?

Not long after that that Sarah and Mickey left the basement unit. Unfortunately when we bought another house our neighbours turned out to be ... you guessed it, Sarah and Mickey.

Sarah's mother, Mary Lou started getting behind in her rent so we had to evict her, but we did succeed in garnisheeing her wages. We managed to recover everything she owed us, including the legal fees.

13

Case X—Bonnie and Clyde

One of our tenants was a character we'll call Clyde. While it's not normally advisable to judge a book by its cover, based on his appearance you might be forgiven for wondering why we would ever have rented to him. We pride ourselves on not pre-judging people, but Clyde had quite a "cover," in more ways than one. He had one real eye and one eye that he could pop out whenever he felt like doing it. Most of the time he had the eye out, which took us a while to get used to. If that wasn't shocking enough, he had tattoos all over his body, and around his good eye and the eye socket he had flames of fire. He was on disability and had a girlfriend named Bonnie. We checked his credit reference and found that he didn't owe anybody any money so we decided to take a chance on him.

One of the first things that happened, soon after Bonnie and Clyde moved into the house, was that the front picture window got broken. We replaced it within a few days. Clyde initially said that some kids were throwing a ball and it went through the window. Surprisingly, that had never happened before. Then, a few weeks later, it happened again. He said the neighbour next door was mad at him and threw a rock through the window. After the window was broken for the second time, Clyde made a wooden cover for the window to protect the glass. It had cutouts in the shape of flames, so you could still see the window through it but it would be difficult for a rock or ball to break the glass again. He paid for the windows to be replaced.

Bonnie and Clyde were our tenants for two years. They always paid their rent and didn't cause too much trouble. Clyde did want the front door and side door replaced by more secure doors. We agreed to pay for the doors and he and his father installed them for us for a small cost. We were pretty sure that he had been running a tattoo business out of our house, but didn't question him about it since Bonnie and Clyde were good tenants in comparison with others we'd had.

Towards the end of his stint with us, Clyde seemed to be having trouble coming up with his rent. There were rumors in the neighborhood that he was letting cats in the house so he could feed them to his pet snake. This was a shock to us, as we didn't even know he had a snake. After they moved out, we did get a call from the city, asking about Clyde and his snake. The official said that he had heard that Clyde had a snake on the premises. We assured him that Clyde was gone and there wasn't any evidence of a snake. Clyde had also told us that someone in the neighborhood had accused him of molesting her daughter. This could be the reason he decided to leave. It seemed that everyone was after him.

Clyde is an example of both the stereotypes and the contradictions we've encountered in dealing with our low-income tenants. On one hand, Clyde's appearance and speech was stereotypical of a biker gang member or other underworld character. On the other hand, he was able to function quite well in the "normal" world, and was certainly non-threatening in his demeanor towards us. Yet, there was evidence of trouble that bubbled up intermittently, such as the neighbours who had a bone to pick with him. We could only speculate about what conflicts he might have had with neighbours or others, or what illegal activities he may have been involved in, but we are firm believers in the saying "where there's smoke there's fire." To some extent, everyone who lives in downtown Windsor is exposed to the kinds of activities that transpire on Windsor's mean streets. Not everyone takes part in drug dealing, theft, vandalism, assault and battery, and other such transgressions, but it's not surprising that a sizeable segment of the downtown population is involved in these illegal activities. To a great degree, the inhabitants and even the police tolerate them. Although they would never admit it, undoubtedly many low-income tenants move frequently simply to stay ahead of someone; a creditor, collection agency, the police, an ex-boyfriend, a drug dealer, or some other potentially deadly enemy.

14

Case XI—Escort Me Out of Here

We were extremely excited. The house we had just inspected was surprisingly nice. It was a clean, renovated duplex with three bedrooms in each unit, and included a finished basement and finished loft in the attic as part of the upper unit. Each of the three units in the house was occupied, and the tenants seemed very nice. We signed an agreement to buy the house, and when we took possession two months later and one week before Christmas, the tenants were still there.

It was our first duplex, and we faced our first minor headache on Christmas day when Diane, the tenant living in the basement unit, called to say that the stove was broken and she couldn't cook her Christmas dinner. We told her that we would send a repairman out as soon as possible, but we probably wouldn't be able to get one for a couple of days because of the holiday. She seemed to take this news fairly well, and called a friend who allowed her to cook at her place (or so she told us).

The next minor upset occurred with the same tenant a few days later. Diane called to say that her toilet wasn't working. We sent out a plumber, paying extra for the service call because it was an emergency call on a holiday. The plumber reported that someone had stuffed a towel into the toilet.

When January 1 came around neither Diane nor the tenant living in the upper unit, named Liz, nor the main unit tenant, named Debra, paid their rent. It didn't take us long to realize that the previous owner had just put the tenants or relatives in as a cover so it looked like the house was rented. When you buy a rental property the tenants have to sign an acknowledgement saying that they are paying rent. In retrospect, we could have investigated to determine if these people were legitimate tenants or just relatives or fake tenants. If so, we could have sued the previous owner of the house for fraud.

One day we went to the house to talk to the tenants. We didn't get any answer by knocking on the front door of the upper unit, so we decided to go up the rear fire escape and knock on the back door. A woman we didn't know opened the back door and we noticed that she was dressed in a short, low-cut camisole. She told us that Liz was home, but she was occupied at the moment. The instant she finished saying this, we noticed a couple coming out of one of the bedrooms. The man headed for the stairs leading to the front door, and the woman, also dressed in a skimpy outfit, turned toward us. It was Liz. It didn't immediately dawn on us what was going on, and we asked Liz if she had her rent. She looked a bit flustered and gave some excuse. We continued to ask Liz when she might have her rent and she continued to make excuses.

We paid Debra a visit as well, in the main floor unit. She said she was finding it hard to pay the rent and the utilities, so we made a deal with her to reduce her rent by $50 a month. Of course we never received any rent from her after that.

Someone tipped us that they thought an escort service was being run out of our house so we decided to hire a private investigator, who reported, not surprisingly, that Liz was working for an escort service. Liz was gone by the end of the month, and we evicted both Diane and Debra. In the space of two months, the house had gone from being fully occupied to empty.

After we had repaired, cleaned and painted the upper unit, we advertised it, and rented it to a pair of young women in their early twenties named Jackie and Dagmar. These two were definitely an improvement over their hooker predecessor. They were strippers, or dancers according to the quaint euphemism used to paper over reality in the sex industry. In any case, they seemed like solid citizens in comparison with Liz. We assumed that they would have no trouble coming up with the rent each month, particularly after Jackie told us that she could easily make $300 in one night at the club.

Trouble raised its ugly head in the first month after Jackie and Dagmar moved in. There was an argument between them that escalated into a fight. Dagmar was close to six feet tall and solidly built, and she pummeled the shorter and more lightly built Jackie, who was taken to the hospital. Jackie had suffered cuts and bruises, but was not seriously hurt. However, Dagmar was charged with assault and also decided to move out of the unit she had been sharing with Jackie.

15

Case XII—Perpetrator as Victim

We had worked hard to repair damage, paint and clean up a large unit consisting of the main floor combined with the basement. With four bedrooms, the apartment would be attractive to a large family, and would bring in up to two hundred dollars extra rent per month compared with a two bedroom unit. Dividing the basement off into a separate unit would have been relatively easy—it had a separate entrance, separate bathroom and kitchen area. This could have generated an additional two or three hundred dollars per month, but that would not have been advisable for two main reasons.

The first concern with a basement apartment is the quality of tenant that can be found to rent it. Our experience with basement-dwellers is particularly negative, and we've concluded that they are not worth the hassle. The other problem is that there are a myriad of rules that have to be satisfied for a basement unit to be legal. Even if a basement unit has passed a building inspection in the recent past, there is no guarantee that it will pass at the next inspection. This can result in having to choose between making thousands of dollars worth of repairs, or closing the unit down. This takes us back to the tenant quality issue, because the nature of the game is such that a tenant will likely call the city building department for an inspection if there is any dispute between the tenant and the landlord.

It was a crisp cold Sunday afternoon in late February. We had been working all weekend to prepare the unit for tenants who would be moving in within a couple of days. Finally, we were finished, except for one small final task. We had brought our camcorder, and performed a ten-minute walkthrough of the unit to record its condition. You can never be too careful.

The new tenants were a middle-aged woman on disability named Jenny and her two children in their late teens, Mike and Leanne. Mike appeared to be about twenty, while Leanne was seventeen or eighteen. They all seemed nice.

Even though we each worked for twenty hours on the weekend, there were still a few minor items to take care of, which we did during visits to the house over the next month. We noticed that Jenny was never around, which aroused our suspicion that she was living somewhere else. There were also a few minor complaints from the new tenants; such as a leaking drainpipe under the shower that was leaking water onto the bathroom floor. Our plumber couldn't find any evidence of a leaking pipe, and told the tenants to make sure the shower door was closed when taking a shower.

The first sign of more serious trouble appeared about four months later. We got a call from Joe, the tenant in the upper unit complaining about noise coming from Jenny's unit. Joe said that a group of Leanne's friends seemed to be visiting most of the time, and they were partying, playing loud music, and yelling. According to Joe, Leanne's brother Mike wasn't happy with the new crowd, so we called Mike and asked him what was going on. Mike said that Leanne was moving out, and he and his mother would be leaving at the end of the month. We told him that provincial law requires them to give us sixty days notice before moving out, but we would waive that requirement as long as Jenny paid the balance owing on her last month's rent, and also gave us a written notice of her intention to vacate.

We never got the written notice. Four weeks later, on a Sunday exactly five months after the video walkthrough, we stopped by the unit and immediately noticed something wrong with the front door. A large beveled plate-glass window in the front door was broken, and the window was boarded-up with what looked like pieces of particleboard shelving. A broken aluminum-framed storm window was sitting nearby on the front porch. The front door was open and we poked our heads inside. There was no sign of anyone there.

We immediately called Jenny and left her a phone message to the effect that she was on record as the official tenant and would be held liable for any damage to the unit. The next morning, we received a phone call from someone who said his name was Oscar, and he was a friend of Jenny. He claimed to own a home renovation business, and stated that he would be going into the unit that afternoon to start repairs. "Hold it," said Charles. "We haven't even had a chance to check the damage ourselves yet."

We agreed to meet Oscar at the house and go over the damage first before discussing the repairs. We realized that he probably couldn't deliver, and might be scamming us, but thought it wouldn't hurt to go along with him on the off chance that he was acceptable.

We waited at the house for Oscar to arrive, and after a few minutes decided to call him. He answered the phone, and immediately apologized for being late.

"I've been up all night," he said. "Leanne was raped last night at a club, and we've been in emergency and talking to the cops. We just got home."

"Listen" said Charles "It sounds like you've got more important things to do than come over to the house, so we can do this in a couple of days."

"It's OK, I'll be there in a few minutes," said Oscar.

When Oscar arrived he explained that he was Jenny's ex-husband, not Leanne and Mike's father, but their stepfather. Really, he was the ex-stepfather. According to Oscar, after Leanne left the club, a man that she had met there followed her, and eventually he raped her. It wasn't too clear to us exactly how it had happened, but we didn't really want to know anyway. Oscar did say that she had also been raped a few months previously, under similar circumstances.

We went through the house with Oscar to inspect the damage, taking notes. Oscar seemed to know a lot about how the damage had occurred. According to him, Mike had invited some of his friends to stay at the house after Jenny and Leanne moved out, and they were responsible for the damage. The beveled glass in the front door had been broken by one of Mike's guests during a drunken fight. Oscar had screwed boards into the door to cover the opening. The guests were also responsible for a number of pizza-sized holes in the walls. Oscar also pointed out that the ceiling fan in the living room wasn't working. Apparently, one of Mike's female guests, who was suicidal, had tried to hang herself from the fan.

After we had gone through the house, we went to a convenience store to make a copy of our notes for Oscar. Oscar said that he was trying to look out for Leanne and Mike even though he wasn't their biological father, and had broken up with Jenny at least ten years earlier. Mike had joined a carnival that was traveling through northwest Ontario to the Manitoba border, and Oscar said that he would make sure that Mike paid for all of the damage. We told Oscar that we wanted to be compensated for all of the materials and labour that we couldn't do ourselves. The main items were the beveled glass, and a carpet in the basement that had been destroyed.

In the end, Oscar never made any firm commitment to pay anything. We tried to call Jenny to discuss the problem, but her cell phone had been disconnected. We got her new number from Oscar, and managed to reach her. She said that most of the damage had been done by one of Mike's guests, and she was going to "nail" him and get the money to pay for the repairs from him.

We never received a cent from Jenny, Mike, or Oscar and had to pay for everything ourselves. We did call disability to apprise them of the situation and let them know that we thought Jenny was living in Detroit. We have no idea whether disability followed up on our advice—they certainly wouldn't discuss it with us.

We've been victimized by a number of tenant scams, two of which
are illustrated by the story of Jenny and her children; we call them "the
neighbour from hell" and "the tenant switch." Below, we've compiled
a summary of the more common tenant scams, including the two used
by Jenny's crowd. We've already described most of these scams in previous chapters. Some are costly to the landlord and others are mostly a
nuisance, but all of them betray a me-first attitude of low-income tenants who are encouraged to view themselves as victims and therefore
entitled to behave in whatever way they want. In most cases, there's not
much that the landlord can do to prevent the scams or get compensation. The scams could be viewed as "the cost of doing business" but the
reality is that they cause huge headaches and make it impossible to earn
a profit. The way that we like to think about most of these scams is that
they are ways of creating negative value. For a variety of reasons it is
advantageous to tenants to damage and destroy property or at least
minimize the economic value of property. Normally, one would imagine that in a functional society there would be an incentive for everyone to create rather than destroy. However, that is clearly not the case
with regard to low-income tenants, and we do not fully grasp why this
is true. Certainly, the fact that these people operate largely outside the
mainstream society and the mainstream economy has a lot to do with
it. Here is a summary of the most significant scams:

- *The neighbour from hell.* This scam occurs when both units of a
  duplex are occupied. It starts with a phone call from one of the
  tenants complaining about the other tenant. Noise is the most
  popular vehicle, but it could be about dope smoking, an intimidating dog, garbage, or any number of irritants. As soon as we
  receive this call, we immediately realize that it is the beginning
  of the end. Both sets of tenants will be leaving soon or will stop
  paying rent and will have to be evicted. It's amazing to realize
  that people who are normally quite happy living in the most
  chaotic of drug-infested circumstances suddenly become deeply
  concerned about their neighbour's pot smoking when it's con-

venient to do so. This particular scam was practiced by Jenny and her neighbour, Joe, as well as by the Fowlers in Chapter 7.

- *The tenant switch.* This scam begins when a very presentable applicant answers a rental ad. The applicant has a good credit record, and is accepted as a tenant. However, the applicant is only a front for a group of typically young, troubled, and drug-infested people who, once they get the keys, invade the property and use it to crash, do drugs, deal drugs, house pit bulls, dump junk, and inevitably damage the property. In Jenny's case, she acted as a front to get her children into our place. Later, the children left, leaving the house to a bunch of young drug addicts. In Chapter 5, Pamela and Bobby were a front for another gang of young, dangerous thugs.

- *Summer in January.* Some tenants seem to want to capture July weather in their unit all year long. They set the thermostat at 30°C during the winter and then watch their kids and boy-friends go shirtless. This only works for the tenant if heating is included in the rent. Carol, who we described in Chapter 6, is a perfect example of someone who perpetrated this scam.

- *The public dump.* For the most part, the furniture and other belongings of low-income tenants are nearly at end-of-life. When a tenant vacates or is evicted, it's more convenient for her to pick up new junk for the new place rather than taking the old junk. At this point, their junk is end-of-life, and it's the respon-sibility of the landlord to dispose of it. The landlord has no con-trol over how much junk the tenant leaves behind, and has no legal means to recover the cost of disposing of it from the ten-ant. Check out the mountain of junk left behind by Stephanie in Chapter 11.

- *The interior decorator (part 1).* Almost every tenant is a closet interior designer with (in his or her mind) superior taste and the talent to improve the look of any apartment. In reality, we've found that a tenant who is allowed to paint will probably make a mess of the job. For example, the tenant will likely simply paint over electrical wall plates, including the plug or switch, rather than going to the effort of removing the plate. Personally, we don't think that wall plates (including the electrical plugs and switches) painted the same colour as the wall are particularly attractive, especially if the colour is lime green. If the wall plates are removed, chances are that the tenant will not replace them. Inevitably, the tenant will then call the city building inspector for an inspection. The building inspector will then issue an order to repair, citing missing cover plates and demanding an expensive inspection by the Electrical Safety Authority.

- *The interior decorator (part 2)*. A rampant scam on the part of tenants is the removal of carpets without the landlord's approval. In some cases, we find a discarded carpet lying in the back yard. In others, the tenant will mention in an unrelated conversation later on that they've removed a carpet, always for a "good reason." Examples include: my roommate is allergic and the carpet traps dust; my dog pissed all over the carpet so I had to remove it (no explanation is given of where the dog is pissing now); I prefer hardwood floors, etc. This scam was perpetrated by Carol in Chapter 6 and by "my bother Darrell" in Chapter 9.

- *The apartment-hunting relative*. This is a variant on the tenant switch. Sometimes, parents or an aunt will make an appointment to view a unit for a prospective tenant. Invariably, these relatives are well spoken, reasonably well educated and project an image of stability and responsibility that tends to lull the landlord into a false sense of security. Just as invariably, the tenant is unstable and irresponsible. Often, as part of this scam, the parent or friend follows up after the tenant moves in. In this case, when the landlord first visits a new tenant's unit, the tenant's parents or friend happen to be there and begin to express concerns about all manner of problems with the unit. Such problems could include:

  - The ducts need to be cleaned because the tenant has allergies

- The carpets need to be cleaned because the tenant has allergies

- It looks like someone broke into the back door and it needs to be replaced

- There's a draft and the windows need to be replaced

- Of course, the tenant turns out to be someone who has a constant stream of visitors at all hours of the night and day, disturbs the neighbours, and locks herself out of the unit, requiring her friends to break down the door.

16

Case XIII—Co-operate or Else

After we rented the main floor unit of the duplex where we had found Mama Mae and her gang (see Chapter 4), we still had to rent the upper unit. We found a nice young couple. John and Ed were very polite, very sincere, and yes, very gay. The tenant in the main floor unit had nothing but nice things to say about them. She admitted that there were times when she forgot to take her clothes out of the dryer and when she went to go and get them, the clothes were folded all nice and neat on top of the dryer. They had flowers planted in flower boxes outside of their door. "Bingo," we thought we hit the jackpot.

The upper unit of this duplex had a metal fire escape. Although the fire escape complied with the building code, it was very high and we were very nervous of it. Therefore we included a clause in the rental agreement that John and Ed signed, whereby they acknowledged that they would not use the fire escape except for emergencies.

One day in late February, we got a call from John. He said he had taken a fall on the fire escape three weeks earlier. He said that he had suffered a broken arm (he described it as shattered) and that he had to have a pin put in his arm. When Eileen asked why he didn't call right away to let us know what had happened, he said he was too laid up. When Eileen asked what he was doing out on the fire escape, he said he was sweeping snow off the landing and accidentally fell down the steps. When Eileen reminded him that he and Ed had signed an agreement saying they would not use the fire escape except for emergency purposes, he paused. He said he didn't remember signing that in the agreement. He asked us to contact our insurance. We refused, on the grounds that he had violated the terms of the rental agreement.

A few days later, we got a letter from John's lawyer threatening to sue us. As a result, we contacted our lawyer and our insurance company, believing that we had a pretty good case. However, once our insurance company got involved the case was taken out of our hands, and the insurance company reached a settlement with John. We were not privy to the details of the settlement, but our insurance premiums didn't increase significantly, so it's likely that John didn't win too much in the case.

Not long after that, John and Ed gave us their notice to vacate the unit. The problem was that they gave us their notice in the middle of the month, so that we had less than sixty days notice. Normally, we might have accepted the notice, but because of the lawsuit we decided not to accept it, and told them to give us a notice for sixty days from the first of the following month. They got upset about that, until they talked to their lawyer and found out that we were right. In the end, we let them leave early, just so that we didn't have to put up with them any more.

17

Case XIV—Madness: Fran Chey

Fran Chey was on disability. Most people picture a disabled person as someone in a wheelchair. However, in the low-income rental business, disability is almost invariably something that is not obviously visible. If you are going to be a client of social services, disability is the way to go. Disability benefits are twice as rich as is welfare for an able-bodied adult with no children. Furthermore, these benefits cannot easily be terminated or the recipient forced to get a job. Some prospective tenants on disability will let you know what their disability is, others won't. Based on our experience, we believe that many of them suffer from bipolar disorder, or at least exhibit the symptoms of bipolar disorder. We think Fran was bipolar. It's usually difficult to get sufficient credit information on prospective tenants who are on disability because they simply have very little credit history, but sometimes we take a chance on one, such as Fran.

We got a call from Fran one morning saying there was a leak coming from the ceiling of her bedroom. She was screaming frantically over the phone, insisting that she wanted to have it fixed "immediately." When we told her that we had to contact our repairman first to see what the problem was, she became even more agitated. Willy arrived at the house within an hour after we got the call, and realized the toilet in the upper unit was leaking. As he was checking out the damage to the bedroom ceiling Fran started hitting him and yelling at him, so he had to leave for his own protection. He called us and told us what had just gone on, saying that as he went out the front door she ran after him, hitting him on his back.

We phoned Fran, but we couldn't calm her down. This incident had made it clear to us that she was seriously ill. We ended up having to hire a security guard to accompany our plumber to the house just to get the toilet fixed.

We had noticed a lot of garbage lying around outside the house and asked if she would please pick it up. She started yelling again and said she was going to call the building department to complain about the house. A building inspector called and asked if we were the owners of the house. When we said yes, he admitted that Fran Chey had called him and said he would let it go as he realized that she was seriously unstable.

We learned later that after she left our unit, Fran set fire to the next place she rented, destroying that house as well as the neighbouring one. Luckily, we only had to deal with the leaking toilet.

18

Case XV—Of Mice and Men: Biff

We first met Biff when he and his wife came to look at an upper unit in one of our houses. We've named him Biff because, as we got to know him, he began to strongly remind us of Michael J. Fox's bullying nemesis from *Back to the Future*.

Biff and his wife liked the unit as it had a finished loft plus two other spacious bedrooms. This particular duplex was about one hundred years old, and at one time it must have been a luxurious house. As a single family home, it would have had five bedrooms upstairs, not counting the loft. The trim and moldings were very old-fashioned. Once, when we removed the ceramic tiles from the shower in the bathroom on the main floor to install a tub surround, we discovered art nouveau wallpaper featuring nude nymphs that must have been quite risqué when it was put up. We thought at one time if we ever made enough money with our rental operation we could probably renovate and possibly put it back into its original state as a single family home.

Things went well with Biff for a while. However, he seemed to be a bully. We could hear him yelling at his wife and little boy occasionally in a very abusive manner. They had moved into our duplex in March and paid an extra $50 per month to cover the hydro expense for a portable air conditioner in the summer, without any complaint. We didn't know that they had gotten a dog. In October, they started complaining about fleas. We told them that there was a clause in the rental agreement they had signed requiring them to follow a flea control program for their pets. We explained that they hadn't complained all summer about fleas, so we felt that their dog had brought the fleas into the house and therefore they would have to pay to have their unit sprayed for fleas. Biff ranted and raved, swearing abusively until we finally gave in and said we would pay for the spraying. In the same conversation he started complaining about the paint job. We told him that he was pushing his luck as we just agreed to pay for spraying.

Biff would also call us at 11:00 p.m. and complain about a dripping faucet. He would undergo a complete personality change, transforming into a raging bully. Then he started complaining about mice. We immediately took care of the mouse problem and reimbursed him for a pillow that he claimed mice had chewed.

Time would go by and then he would complain about mice again. We noticed that Biff and his wife wouldn't store their garbage in proper containers. When we mentioned the rental agreement they had signed, requiring them to keep garbage in proper containers, he would rant and rave again. The harassment was beginning to be too much to deal with. They also stopped paying for air conditioning the following summer.

One weekend when Eileen was painting the lower unit she could hear a motor running upstairs in Biff's unit. At first Eileen thought it was a vacuum cleaner, but began to realize it was a much stronger sounding motor. She was alone in the unit she was painting; otherwise she would have confronted Biff. Later in the day, Biff was giving his two-year-old boy rides up and down the street on a mini motorcycle commonly called a pocket bike. He would also gun the motor on the front porch right by the front door of the unit that Eileen was working in. Eileen then realized that the motor she had heard upstairs was from the pocket bike. The little boy had been upstairs with him, breathing in the exhaust fumes from the motor.

We continued to see Biff with his little boy, whipping down the street at a high speed. The neighbours told us that the police and children's aid had already been called in the past about Biff's joy rides with the boy. One neighbour also complained that Biff had waved a knife at her little girl for doing something that had irritated him.

Biff had an anxiety about mice that we thought was probably a phobia. Several months would pass without any complaints and then he would call, often in the middle of the night, insisting that, "You've got to do something about these fucking mice." Biff would work himself into a frenzy, becoming louder and louder and making it impossible to get a word in edgewise. Finally, after five or ten minutes Biff's ranting and raving would subside and we could say something. We would call a pest control company to set up an appointment to visit Biff's unit. However, sometimes he wouldn't answer the door when the exterminators arrived, and another appointment would have to be arranged. Once the problem was taken care of, the complaints would cease for a few more months. Upon visiting his unit we found that his garbage still wasn't in closed containers.

Biff began to insist that mice were getting into the house through spaces between the bricks where the mortar had eroded. He kept saying that the foundation of the house was crumbling. When a leak occurred in his front hall, he decided that it was due to rain getting into the wall through cracks between the bricks. We contracted a roofer, who said that the leak was due to a missing flashing between the two-storey house and the single storey extension containing the front hall. The roofer said that Biff's theory about rain leaking through the bricks was ludicrous, since the walls of the hundred-year old house were double-brick with wooden planks between the bricks.

We called the pest control company to make an appointment to visit Biff's unit, but he never answered the phone or replied to the phone messages they left, so they were unable to get into his place for over two months. When we told Biff we would like to accompany the exterminator on a visit to his unit, he said that he didn't want them there any more.

After listening to Biff's complaints on and off for two years, we were taken by surprise when he called one day and offered to buy the house, albeit for a lowball amount. We said that if we were to list it for sale with a realtor, the asking price would be thirty thousand dollars more than what he offered, but for a private sale we could bring that down by five thousand dollars. We also asked him to make an offer in writing if he was serious about buying the house. He started arguing that the foundation was crumbling.

We didn't hear from Biff for a few days. Then he called and began complaining about mice again. He told Eileen that he was going to call the city building department. That was the last straw. We had put up with his dog digging holes in the front yard while tied to a banister inside the front door with the rope going out the front door (leaving the door open about an inch), windows left open in the winter, foul language, abusive behaviour to his wife and son as well as to ourselves, so Eileen said "Well there's a few people we can call too, Biff."

That was it! He said, "You're threatening me." Eileen told him that the neighbours had told us children's aid had already been called and that we could follow up.

Biff filed applications with the Tribunal alleging maintenance problems and harassment, apparently without any legal assistance. However, he realized that he wasn't going to succeed, and signed a mutual agreement to leave the unit by the end of the month. The weekend after he moved out we came to check his unit and found water overflowing from the sinks in the kitchen and bathroom.

Someone had broken a window to get in, had plugged the drains and turned on the taps.

The water that had overflowed from the kitchen sink, bathroom sink, bathroom tub, and loft sink leaked through to the stairwell, going down to the main unit. The drywall in the ceiling over the stairwell came loose and fell onto the stairs. The carpets upstairs, as well as the carpet on the stairs, would have to be replaced.

Our feeling was one of complete disdain for this person. We called the police, but they said that unless we had proof that Biff did it they couldn't do anything. The idea that he would do all of these things just because we refused to sell the house to him for the price he wanted was unbelievable.

We feel sure that, one of these days, Biff will be in the news.

Garbage dumped at the back door by Biff.

Biff's pocket bike.

We found the sinks overflowing after Biff moved out.

Broken glass from a window used by someone to break in after Biff moved out.

Drywall on the back stairs, fallen from the ceiling, resulting from the flood in Biff's unit.

19

Fighting Back

In this book, we've described the systemic abuse of landlords perpetrated under the landlord-tenant system by the "special welfare cult" and its clients, the recipients of social services. The key to the success of these scams is the secrecy with which the welfare system is operated. This cloak of secrecy hides the arbitrariness, abuse, and even corruption that benefit the initiated. In turn, the flourishing of the system drives a need for even more secrecy.

In Chapter 1 we described the systemic problems of the Ontario welfare and landlord-tenant systems that allow low-income tenants to take advantage of landlords. In Chapter 8 we explored the background to the current situation in Windsor that is aggravating the problem. However, we have to admit that in spite of several years' experience dealing with social services and the Tribunal *cum* Board, not to mention Windsor Police, Windsor Building Department, Fire, ESA, etc, we still have an inadequate grasp of how the system works.

It's not for lack of trying that we haven't been able to piece the puzzle together. Perhaps we haven't been asking the right questions. We'll leave that judgment to the readers of this book, but before that judgment is rendered, we would like to describe our attempts to learn more.

One approach we have taken is to contact City of Windsor councilors on the premise that they ultimately run social services and therefore must be knowledgeable. A city councilor may not have time to explain it, but it would be reasonable to assume that a councilor would be able to direct questions to an appropriate city staff member.

Charles initiated a dialogue with Caroline Postma and Ron Jones, the Windsor Ward 2 councilors, with an e-mail on May 20, 2006. The idea at that time was simply to alert the councilors to the ongoing deterioration of downtown Windsor (something that is virtually self-evident) and to bring forward an idea for improvement. Ron Jones called back almost immediately and left a message. Charles e-mailed Ron Jones thanking him for responding so quickly and asking him to call again. However, he didn't call, or at least never left a message.

Charles tried again with a phone call to Caroline Postma in June, 2006. Ms. Postma seemed quite interested in what Charles had to say, and the conversation lasted for the better part of an hour. Regarding crime, she said that city council would be committing additional police to patrol the downtown. To improve the downtown environment, she said that a study of the situation had been performed and would be followed up. Regarding the difficult rental market, she said that she was working on getting tax breaks for owners of rental properties to perform the renovations needed to convert them to single-family homes.

Caroline Postma said that operating rules for Windsor social services are available to the public, and that audits are held regularly and are also available. In particular, Caroline Postma promised to contact appropriate city staff to provide us with information about the plans for the downtown core and about the workings of the social services department.

Soon afterward, we received an e-mail from Jim Yanchula on June 30, 2006 with links to studies that had been performed to revitalize the downtown core. Essentially, the key strategy is to establish an "urban village," something that has been tried elsewhere.

A month passed and we received no information on welfare, so we sent Caroline Postma another e-mail on August 12, 2006 reminding her that she had promised to send information, and posing specific questions. As of publication, we have still received no reply.

So far, our experience in getting information about the operations of the social services department in Windsor has been disappointing, if not surprising. We've learned nothing. There may be consultants out there who are willing to divulge information for a sizeable fee, but why should we have to resort to that? There are a few basic principles about this that we think are obvious. However, we have no evidence that any of them are being followed:

- As for any major organization, public or private, Windsor social services must be operated according to written policies and procedures.

- The organization must be subject to audits to determine whether the procedures are, in fact, being followed. Audits should identify corrective actions to be taken in the event that a nonconformance is identified.

- Policies, procedures and audit findings for a public organization such as Windsor social services should be available to the public.

- The information has to be available to everyone without the need to take special measures, such as Access to Information, special consultants, etc.

We are not asking for information about specific welfare cases. However, there have to be policies and procedures that govern how welfare clients are handled, including how much discretion on the part of caseworkers and their superiors is authorized.

Let us be even more clear that as long as this information is not forthcoming to us, our suspicion grows that a secretive "special welfare cult" exists for the benefit of those who run it. Questions that arise include:

- Are large rental property owners in Windsor also major city council campaign contributors? Are these major landlords also privy to information emanating from social services, or special favours, that small landlords cannot get?

- An audit of CAS by the Ontario auditor found that there have been widespread examples of delays in dealing with problems that could put children at risk, while at the same time, there have been widespread abuses of travel privileges, auto expenses, etc. Is it possible that similar, or more severe abuses are occurring within social services organizations throughout the province? It is undeniable that the seeds for such a situation were sewn when Mike Harris downloaded the responsibility for welfare to the municipalities. With a multitude of municipal social service departments throughout the province, there is bound to be a wide variability in the way they are run.

Our suspicions about improper activity at social services are heightened by the secrecy with which the department is operated. As we have explained, we have been unable to obtain any information about the operation of social services. The agency acts almost as though it were a private company trying to protect some super secret commercial information against industrial espionage perpetrated by competitors. Perhaps the covert operations of a biker gang or terrorist cell would be a more accurate analogy. However, we'll stick with the cult comparison we've used in our title. One wonders what the organization in general, and its employees in particular, have to hide.

An inherent aspect of the culture of secrecy at social services is arrogance in dealing with "outsiders." The receptionist dismisses telephone inquiries with disdain. "Our staff don't take calls from landlords" is the blunt response to a request to talk to a tenant's worker about an issue of concern. Because of this, we have taken to a little subterfuge when phoning social services. Generally Eileen makes the call, and neglects to mention that she is a landlord. Often, it appears that the receptionist assumes that she is a social services "client" and transfers the call to the social worker.

Based on our experience, the high-handed attitude of social services staff applies to all dealings with landlords. For example, in the case of Stephanie we described in Chapter 11, we had arranged to have her rent paid directly to us by social services on the first of each month. We received a cheque on schedule at the start of her second month, but did not get the third month's payment on time. After a couple of days, we phoned our tenant Stephanie and asked her if she knew what had happened to the rent payment. She said that, for some reason, social services had deposited the rent money in her bank account, and she would pay the rent as soon as possible. As we've said in Chapter 11, the reality was that she asked social services to terminate the direct pay agreement that they had with us, and they readily complied. We received a letter from social services a few days later stating bluntly that they were terminating the direct payments, without any explanation.

Social workers have tried to excuse their attitude by saying that their job is to deal with their clients, not landlords or other outsiders. We find this infuriating for a number of reasons. Firstly, the use of the word "client" to describe social services recipients bears no similarity to the meaning of the word in any other context. A client is someone who has a business arrangement with someone else, whereby the client pays the other party for a service. By this logic, social services recipients should be paying their workers for some service they are providing. As far as we know, social services recipients are not paying their social workers, although we cannot prove that it is not happening. We don't suppose that social services would want anyone to suspect that "clients" are actually paying workers. Therefore, why would they use such a loaded term? Perhaps it came into use as a euphemism designed to confer respectability or status on social services recipients. The problem with misusing language to turn logic on its head is that this technique is commonly used as a propaganda/brainwashing tool. The seemingly well meaning, but Orwellian, tactic of twisting the meaning of "client" has become a tool to rebuff inquiries or investigations by outsiders. As in "We only deal with clients," and the implied, "How dare you interfere with our work to help our poor clients?"

The other aspect that is even more infuriating is the idea that the information lane between landlords and social workers must be a one-way street. Landlords are to speak only when they are spoken to. Social services policies, such as the provision of startup fees, direct pay, and one-year leases directly affect landlords, usually not for the better.

On another front, we tried to get our message through to the Ontario minister of Municipal Affairs and Housing on the issue of tenant evictions and the need for reform of the landlord-tenant legislation. As we noted in Chapter 1, in the spring of 2006 tenant groups blitzed the media with stories of a massive increase in tenant evictions and a demand for tighter rules to minimize evictions. We've detailed throughout this book how the vast majority of evictions are initiated for deliberate nonpayment of rent, and how eviction benefits the tenant and not the landlord in most cases. What is needed to address this situation is legislation to prevent tenants from getting something for nothing. We wrote to the housing minister to explain this. He responded by asserting "both landlords and tenants have faced difficulties under the current law," and promising legislation that would "improve fairness in the dispute-resolution process, and would encourage the proper maintenance and growth of rental housing across the province." However, he chose to listen to the tenant groups and ignore our message, by introducing legislation to increase the period of time that a tenant is permitted to live rent-free before being evicted, and to allow tenants to raise maintenance issues at eviction hearings for nonpayment of rent.

We have spent several years trying to analyze the situation and have concluded that the triangular relationship between low-income tenants, their landlords and the "system" reflects and is subject to more general trends occurring in society. On one hand is the conflict between individual and group rights, and justice. The *Charter of Rights and Freedoms* represents the apex of group rights, and to a large extent continues to provide the philosophical guidance for landlord-tenant rules. In this context, tenants can be seen a group, and therefore each tenant belonging to the group possesses inherent rights. Landlords on the other hand are individuals and therefore not possessing rights. However, the ascendancy of the faith-based political right in both the

US and Canada has brought, at least superficially, an emphasis on individual rights and responsibility, underpinned by an absolute morality. This would suggest that tenants should be held to account, if not by society then by their landlords. However, society does not hold tenants to account and landlords are not permitted to do so. If a tenant does not pay her rent, a landlord is not permitted to change the locks.

One could imagine that legislation that balances the rights of landlords and tenants would permit the landlord to change the locks, and would allow the tenant to sue for wrongful eviction (i.e., if she actually did pay her rent). Such legislation would impose stiff penalties against any landlord found guilty of wrongdoing. However, this eminently logical approach is not followed. Does this mean that the right wing revolution has not yet begun to influence landlord-tenant rules, at least not in Ontario? Has politics trumped ideology? There is undoubtedly some truth to this, but it also appears that the issue of landlord's rights, and particularly the rights of small landlords, is of limited interest to the right wing ideologues. Yes, they are concerned with the need for everyone to take personal responsibility, and have cut welfare payments accordingly. However, large landlords are not in any danger of going out of business under the current system. If worst comes to worst, they can always convert their buildings to condominiums. However, the small landlord is left to fend for himself.

Ironically, the right wing trend to free markets and individual rights has had a significant impact on society in general, and has clearly resulted in a growing disparity between high-income and low-income people. As it becomes increasingly difficult for low-income tenants to support themselves, governments will continue to increase pressure on small landlords to make up the difference. It has been, and will continue to be easy for politicians of every stripe to convince themselves that small landlords have a primary responsibility to their tenants. This is clearly true for left-leaning politicians, but is just as attractive to right wingers who may see it as an expression of morality. After all, landlords generally are considered to be people of some means who have taken on their responsibilities voluntarily. Meanwhile, the responsibility imputed to tenants, i.e. the requirement to pay their rent and refrain from damaging their rental unit will continue to weaken as their ability to pay is eroded.

Action to address the problems we've exposed needs to begin at the grassroots level. It is our hope that the stories and analysis we've presented in this book will resonate with the many small landlords in Ontario and throughout Canada. Ideally, it will help to galvanize the political action that is needed to rebalance the political scales. Fairminded members of the public, who may not have been aware just how skewed the system is, are also likely to be a significant source of support for change.

Concrete action is needed on a number of fronts. Specific measures that concerned citizens should support and lobby for include:

- As a first step towards the goal of restoring fairness and accountability to the social welfare system, the provincial auditor should perform an audit of the system. Ideally, the audit would cover all of the agencies in Ontario, but if a partial audit is performed (similar to that done for children's aid) the city of Windsor should be included.

- An audit is a necessary element but not sufficient to reveal all of the problems in the system. The reason for this is that the objective of an audit is to determine whether policies and procedures are in place, and whether they are being followed (as evidenced by a "paper trail"). In other words, an audit can determine if there are rules and whether the rules are followed, but is not primarily concerned with the legitimacy of the rules. Therefore, a more fundamental review of the system is required at the political level. The review should allow for meaningful input from directly affected groups such as small landlords who have been effectively shut out in the past.

- Where are the enterprising investigative journalists that the major newspapers like to brag about? It would be far easier for a journalist to investigate problems in the social welfare system than for a small landlord operating on a shoestring. Our experience tells us that this is low-hanging fruit; a topic that has not enjoyed any scrutiny but is bound to reveal plenty of attention-grabbing discoveries with little effort. Politicians and social service functionaries cannot afford to stonewall the news media as easily as they have stonewalled us. There is no excuse for the media to continue to ignore this issue. Action should start with an investigation of Windsor social services by the *Windsor Star*.

Once the public is made aware of the reality of Ontario's social welfare system, pressure for change will grow. The politicians will be forced to respond. In addition to getting operations cleaned up at municipal social service agencies, specific reforms need to be implemented, as detailed in Chapter 1:

- Legislation should be amended to allow landlords to garnishee social service payments.

- Landlord-tenant rules that allow tenants to live rent-free for two months should be scrapped.

- Start-up fees for welfare recipients who deliberately stop paying rent should be scrapped.

- The fee to file applications with the Landlord and Tenant Board should be the same for landlords and tenants.

- Landlords should be allowed to collect a cleaning/damage deposit.

Recently, tenant groups have called for licensing of landlords, ostensibly to ensure that minimum maintenance standards are met. This approach is clearly applicable to tenants as well. To ensure that tenants meet minimum standards with respect to the issues explored in this book, such as non-payment of rent, disturbing or harassing neighbours or the landlord, and damaging property, we recommend that:

- A licensing body should be set up, including representation from small landlords, to license tenants.

To rebalance landlord-tenant legislation, political pressure needs to be applied to the provincial housing minister to amend the Residential Tenancies Act. We have tried to educate the housing minister, to no avail (see above). He ignored us not because we were wrong, but because we have no political clout. The landlord-tenant issue differs from the social welfare problem in that the main culprit is the legislation itself, rather than the way it is implemented. Although there are undoubtedly activist adjudicators who habitually side with tenants in landlord-tenant disputes, the legislation is already so one-sided that adjudicator bias hardly makes a difference. While investigative journalism has a role to play, it is unlikely to be a prime mover of public opinion in this case. Organized lobbying by small landlords is needed, but perhaps even more important will be the natural market response to the situation. As small and large landlords pull out of the rental business in response to the unfavourable business environment, government will be forced to provide housing for the least desirable tenants. Government will likely respond by passing more balanced legislation to entice small landlords back into the market.

The consequences of not rebalancing the social welfare and landlord-tenant systems will, ironically, be a deterioration in support for low-income Ontarians by the middle class majority, as well as increasing cynicism about the role of government. This will lead, on one hand, to increased drug-related crime, homelessness, violence, and ultimately class strife between middle-income and low-income Ontarians. On the other hand, support for government action to ensure social justice will wane.

We hope that this book will be viewed by the media, the public, and by politicians as a call to action. If it is not, we are not optimistic about the social and economic future of Ontario.

March 2, 2006

John Gerretsen, Minister
Municipal Affairs and Housing
777 Bay Street, 17'th Floor
Toronto, Ontario M5G 2E5

Dear Sir:

We are writing because of recent news articles about tenant evictions in Ontario and statements you are reported to have made about pending landlord-tenant legislation. As small landlords, we are concerned that the rationale for change is being based on distortions of reality that are not in the best interests of Ontarians.

We have owned rental properties in Windsor, Ontario since 1996, with 13 rental units in total. We think that our experience and viewpoint is typical of many small landlords, and should be accounted for in preparing legislation. This experience is certainly not what you have heard from tenants organizations, or even from landlords organizations. Since the focus of the news articles is the number of evictions, we will focus on this issue.

As a small landlord in downtown Windsor, all of our tenants have low income, and a majority are clients of Social Services. Every year, it becomes necessary for us to evict one or more tenants. Evictions have been portrayed as good tenants losing their homes at the whim of a landlord, but our experience has been the polar opposite of this picture. Every eviction that we have initiated has been for nonpayment of rent, and we are convinced that in the vast majority of cases the tenant has deliberately withheld rent, not because he or she was unable to pay, but because the legal and social services system provides an incentive to do so. In short, these tenants benefit financially from being evicted. We seriously doubt that any of these evicted tenants was unable to find a home

A tenant benefits from eviction because under the mandated eviction process, he or she can live rent-free for the two months that the eviction process typically takes (we can provide detailed documentation of this time period). Social Services benefits because, if their clients are saving on rent, Social Services payments can be trimmed. In effect, landlords are subsidizing both tenants and Social Services through the eviction process.

In Windsor, Social Services also provides a "start up fee" to tenants who have been evicted. Tenants have to be evicted to receive this payment - another incentive to stop paying rent. Given the advantages of stopping rent payments it's surprising that more tenants don't engage in the practice.

Letter to the Ontario minister of Municipal Affairs and Housing, explaining why landlord-tenant legislation should not be changed to make eviction of tenants for non-payment of rent more difficult.

We do not bother trying to recover the unpaid rent from an evicted tenant because it is impossible to do so. There is no legal means to enforce a judgment against a client of social services. Typically, our financial losses in this situation include two months rent, Tribunal application fee of $150.00, Sheriff's fee of $325.00 (which is paid whether or not the Sheriff attends an eviction) plus any damage repairs, hauling the tenant's junk to the dump, etc.

The suggestion put forward by some tenant's advocates that landlords are taking advantage of legislation that is tilted in favour of landlords is, based on our experience, preposterous. There is a good reason why landlords apply to evict a tenant who has stopped paying her rent. If he doesn't do so, the tenant will almost certainly continue living rent-free until the landlord takes action. Tenants understand this perfectly well, and they fully expect to be evicted after they stop paying rent.

If, as all reports suggest, you introduce legislation to lengthen the eviction process, it will clearly only exacerbate the currently inequitable system that rewards tenants for unethical behaviour and indirectly penalizes the good tenants who refuse to take advantage of the landlord just because the system allows them to do it. We can only hope that your intention is, instead, to minimize the conditions that encourage tenants to deliberately withhold rent.

We would also like to remind you that, while the difficulties experienced by landlords in Toronto due to the vacancy rate are well-publicized, those problems are trivial compared to the situation in Windsor. The most recent CMHC survey found the vacancy rate in Windsor to be 10.3%, and we can assure you that the vacancy rate for affordable housing such as ours is actually much higher than this. Suggestions that landlords are evicting tenants in Windsor to raise rents would be laughable if they weren't so painful.

To summarize, we are asking you to consider the facts when drafting new landlord-tenant legislation. Do you want to exacerbate the already inequitable situation that rewards unethical behaviour by a minority of tenants, puts the onus for subsidizing tenants who cannot afford their home squarely on the shoulders of landlords, and penalizes good tenants? Or do you want to encourage tenants to take pride in meeting their obligations and taking personal responsibility for their actions?

Sincerely,

Letter to the Ontario minister of Municipal Affairs and Housing, explaining why landlord-tenant legislation should not be changed to make eviction of tenants for non-payment of rent more difficult (continued).

**Minister of Municipal Affairs
and Housing**

777 Bay Street, 17ᵗʰ Floor
Toronto ON M5G 2E5
Tel. (416) 585-7000
Fax (416) 585-6470
www.mah.gov.on.ca

**Ministre des Affaires municipales
et du Logement**

777, rue Bay, 17ᵉ étage
Toronto ON M5G 2E5
Tél. (416) 585-7000
Téléc (416) 585-6470
www.mah.gov.on.ca

Ontario

06-25512

March 27, 2006

Dear Mr. and Ms.

Thank you for your letter of March 2, 2006 in which you express reservations about the introduction of new legislation and relate your experiences as a landlord.

Let me assure you that our government understands that both landlords and tenants have faced difficulties under the current law. We have committed to introducing legislation to replace the *Tenant Protection Act, 1997* with fair and effective tenant/landlord protection. We are aiming for a new system that provides real and balanced protection for landlords and tenants. The new legislation would also improve fairness in the dispute-resolution process, and would encourage the proper maintenance and growth of rental housing across the province.

The introduction of new legislation will come only after a lengthy and open consultation process in which we received valuable input from the people of Ontario.

I appreciate your concern for this matter and would like to thank you again for adding your voice to this important discussion.

Sincerely,

John Gerretsen
Minister

1322(06/96)

Form letter in response from the minister of Municipal Affairs and Housing.

Afterword—Where There's Smoke, There's Fire

Well, here we are at the end of our book. We were wondering how we could conclude our story about our experiences in the rental business with a climactic end. We've told you about a variety of tenants we've had over the years. We've had quite a few characters to reflect on. In Chapter 18 we told you about Biff and how we think that, one day, he could be in the news: we'll let you be the judge.

On a Wednesday morning, around 8:30 a.m., we answered a phone call from the Windsor police. Without any explanation the dispatcher informed us that, "Your house needs to be boarded up immediately!" When we asked why, she said there had been a fire. When we asked how could that be as the house was vacant, she said the fire had started at the house next door and spread to our house. When we asked which house next door—to the left or to the right of us—she said she was only the dispatcher and couldn't tell us, as she didn't know. We then talked to the detective on the case and he said the fire started at 1:00 a.m. in our house and was a case of arson.

The investigators found evidence of Molotov cocktails—more than one. We couldn't believe what we were being told. After hearing the bad news, our thoughts turned to Biff (see Chapter 18). It was the same house that he had lived in. Charles took off for Windsor that morning to see how much damage had been done to our property. Luckily, nobody had been hurt.

Could Biff have done this? We suspected he had turned on the taps and left them running. We have no proof that he did it, but it happened the weekend after he moved out.

We don't know if the police will find out who set the fire before we've published this book, but it certainly has given us a climactic ending to our book. Has everything gone up in smoke? We are survivors. We are trying to do our best, but it would help if more landlords would come forward and tell their stories. Things have got to change.

The finished loft in Biff's unit, after the fire.

About the Authors

Charles Arthur and Eileen Gwyneth Roy are pseudonyms. The authors deemed it necessary to conceal their identities for their own protection. They will possibly reveal their identities at a later time.

Charles Arthur holds a doctorate from the University of Toronto. He is currently employed as an engineer with a well-known Canadian company.

Eileen Gwyneth Roy is not only Dr. Arthur's wife but also his business partner. Together, with their experience in the rental business, they came to the realization that the Ontario government is mismanaging taxpayer's money, and small landlords are being used to subsidize the welfare system. They felt it necessary to document their experience and provide an analysis of the problem.

Index

978-0-595-45103-6
0-595-45103-9